GAO

Report to the Chairman of the Committee on Transportation and Infrastructure, House of Representatives

December 2012

SCREENING PARTNERSHIP PROGRAM

TSA Should Issue More Guidance to Airports and Monitor Private versus Federal Screener Performance

G A O
Accountability ★ Integrity ★ Reliability

GAO-13-208

GAO

Accountability * Integrity * Reliability

Highlights

Highlights of GAO-13-208, a report to the Chairman of the Committee on Transportation and Infrastructure, House of Representatives

SCREENING PARTNERSHIP PROGRAM

TSA Should Issue More Guidance to Airports and Monitor Private versus Federal Screener Performance

Why GAO Did This Study

TSA maintains a federal workforce to screen passengers and baggage at the majority of the nation's commercial airports, but also oversees a workforce of private screeners at airports who participate in the SPP. The SPP allows commercial airports to use private screeners, provided that the level of screening matches or exceeds that of federal screeners. In recent years, TSA's SPP has evolved to incorporate changes in policy and federal law, prompting enhanced interest in measuring screener performance. GAO was asked to examine the (1) status of SPP applications and airport operators', aviation stakeholders', and TSA's reported advantages and disadvantages of participating in the SPP; (2) extent to which TSA has provided airports guidance to govern the SPP application process; and (3) extent to which TSA assesses and monitors the performance of private and federal screeners. GAO surveyed 28 airport operators that had applied to the SPP as of April 2012, and interviewed 5 airport operators who have not applied and 1 airport operator who applied to the SPP after GAO's survey. Although not generalizable, these interviews provided insights. GAO also analyzed screener performance data from fiscal years 2009-2011. This is a public version of a sensitive report that GAO issued in November 2012. Information that TSA deemed sensitive has been redacted.

What GAO Recommends

GAO recommends that the TSA Administrator develop guidance for SPP applicants and a mechanism to monitor private versus federal screener performance. TSA concurred with the recommendations.

View GAO-13-208. For more information, contact Steve Lord at (202) 512-4379 or lords@gao.gov.

What GAO Found

Since implementation of the Screening Partnership Program (SPP) in 2004, 29 airports have applied to the program, citing various advantages and relatively few disadvantages. Of the 25 approved, 16 are participating in the program, 6 are currently in the contractor procurement process, and the remainder withdrew from participation because their commercial airline services were discontinued. In 2011, the Transportation Security Administration (TSA) denied applications for 6 airports because, according to TSA officials, the airports did not demonstrate that participation in the program would "provide a clear and substantial advantage to TSA security operations." After enactment of the Federal Aviation Administration Modernization and Reform Act of 2012 (FAA Modernization Act) in February 2012, TSA revised its SPP application, removing the "clear and substantial advantage" question. Four of the 6 airports that had been denied in 2011 later reapplied and were approved. In GAO's survey and in interviews with airport operators (of SPP and non-SPP airports) and aviation stakeholders, improved customer service and increased staffing flexibilities were most commonly cited as advantages or potential advantages of the SPP. Individual Federal Security Directors we interviewed cited reduced involvement in human resource management as an advantage; however, TSA generally remains neutral regarding the SPP. Few disadvantages were cited; however, some airport operators cited satisfaction with federal screeners and concerns with potential disruption from the transition to private screening services.

TSA has developed some resources to assist SPP applicants; however, it has not provided guidance to assist airports applying to the program. Consistent with the FAA Modernization Act, TSA's revised SPP application requested that applicants provide information to assist TSA in determining if their participation in the SPP would compromise security or detrimentally affect the cost-efficiency or screening effectiveness of passengers and property at their airport. TSA also developed responses to frequently asked questions and has expressed a willingness to assist airports that need it. However, TSA has not issued guidance to assist airports with completing applications and information on how the agency will assess them. Three of five airport operators who applied using the current application stated that additional guidance is needed to better understand how to respond to the new application questions. Developing guidance could better position airports to evaluate whether they are good candidates for the SPP.

TSA recently improved its screener performance measures, but could benefit from monitoring private versus federal screener performance. In April 2012, TSA added measures to ensure that the set of measures it uses to assess screener performance at private and federal airports better addresses its airport screening strategic goals and mission. However, TSA does not monitor private screener performance separately from federal screener performance. Instead, TSA conducts efforts to monitor screener performance at individual SPP airports, but these efforts do not provide information on SPP performance as a whole or across years, which makes it difficult to identify program trends. A mechanism to consistently monitor SPP versus non-SPP performance would better position TSA to ensure that the level of screening services and protection provided at SPP airports continues to match or exceed the level provided at non-SPP airports, thereby ensuring that SPP airports are operating as intended.

_____ **United States Government Accountability Office**

Contents

Figures

Abbreviations

ACI-NA	Airport Council International-North America
AIT	advanced imaging technology
ASAP	Aviation Security Assessment Program
ATSA	Aviation Transportation Security Act
DHS	Department of Homeland Security
EDS	explosives detection system
ETD	explosives trace detection machine
FAA	Federal Aviation Administration
FAQ	frequently asked question
FSD	Federal Security Director
GPRA	Government Performance and Results Act
IPT	Integrated Project Team
MOR	Management Objective Report
NDF	National Deployment Force
OSO	Office of Security Operations
PACE	Presence, Advisement, Communication, and Execution
PMO	Program Management Office
PMR	performance management review
SAC chair	SPP Application Chair
SPP	Screening Partnership Program
TIP	threat image protection
TSA	Transportation Security Administration

United States Government Accountability Office
Washington, DC 20548

December 6, 2012

The Honorable John Mica
Chairman
Committee on Transportation and Infrastructure
House of Representatives

Dear Chairman Mica:

The Transportation Security Administration (TSA) is responsible for ensuring the security of the traveling public through, among other things, screening passengers traveling by aircraft for explosives and other prohibited items. To fulfill this responsibility, TSA maintains a federal workforce of screeners at a majority of the nation's commercial airports, but also oversees a smaller workforce of private screeners employed by companies under contract to TSA at airports that participate in TSA's Screening Partnership Program (hereafter referred to as the SPP, or the Program).[1] The SPP, established in 2004 in accordance with provisions of the Aviation Transportation Security Act (ATSA), allows commercial airports an opportunity to "opt out" of federal screening by applying to TSA to have private-sector screeners perform the screening function.[2] At private screening airports, TSA continues to be responsible for overseeing airport screening operations and ensuring that the contractors provide effective and efficient security operations in a manner consistent with law and other TSA requirements; however, the screening of

---

[1]For purposes of this report, a "commercial airport" is any airport in the United States that operates pursuant to a TSA-approved security program in accordance with 49 C.F.R. pt. 1542 and at which TSA performs or oversees the performance of screening services. Federal screeners employed by TSA are also known as Transportation Security Officers. For the purposes of this report, we refer to screeners at airports that participate in the Screening Partnership Program as "private screeners" and screeners at airports not participating in the Screening Partnership Program as "federal screeners."

[2]See Pub. L. No. 107-71, § 108, 115 Stat. 597, 611-13 (2001) (codified as amended at 49 U.S.C. §§ 44919-20). TSA established the SPP in 2004 after concluding a 2-year pilot program through which four private screening companies performed screening operations at five commercial airports (one contractor served two airports).

GAO-13-208 Screening Partnership Program

passengers and baggage at these airports is performed by private screening contractors selected and approved by the TSA.[3]

Questions about the cost-effectiveness and screening efficiency of private screeners compared with that of federal screeners have increased scrutiny of the SPP. Some representatives of the aviation industry and certain airport operators contend that the SPP capitalizes on the private sector's innovation and flexibility to provide screening services more efficiently and with enhanced customer service. However, the SPP model allows for little variance in screening operations at SPP airports. For example, in accordance with ATSA, private screeners must meet the same standards and requirements for hiring and training that apply to federal screeners, abide by the same standard operating procedures, and be provided compensation and benefits at a level not less than their federal counterparts.[4]

As of January 2011, 16 airports were participating in the SPP.[5] In January 2011, the TSA Administrator announced his decision not to expand the SPP beyond the 16 participating airports "unless a clear and substantial advantage to do so emerges in the future." In so doing, the Administrator cited his interest in helping the agency evolve into a "more agile, high-performing organization that can meet the security threats of today and the future" as the reason for his decision. Of the 6 airports that submitted applications from March 2009 through January 2012 that were evaluated under the "clear and substantial advantage" standard, TSA approved the application of 1 airport, West Yellowstone Airport, and denied the applications of the other 5 airports. According to TSA officials, however, the Federal Aviation Administration (FAA) Modernization and Reform Act of 2012 (FAA Modernization Act), enacted in February 2012, prompted TSA to change the standard by which it evaluates SPP applications and requires, among other things, that the TSA Administrator approve an SPP

---

[3]Private screening airports are airports that are participating in the SPP, also referred to as SPP airports.

[4]See 49 U.S.C. § 44920(c), (f). See also § 44935 (requiring the Administrator to prescribe employment standards and training requirements for, among others, airport security personnel).

[5]In addition to the 16 airports, TSA approved the applications of 3 other airports (including one heliport) prior to January 2011 that are not participating in the program because commercial airline services at these airports were terminated.

GAO-13-208 Screening Partnership Program

application submitted by an airport operator if the Administrator determines that the approval would not compromise security or detrimentally affect the cost-efficiency or the effectiveness of the screening of passengers or property at the airport.[6]

Citing the recent SPP airport approvals, the Committee on Appropriations, House of Representatives, recommended approximately $160 million for privatized screening for fiscal year 2013, which represents $15 million above the amount requested in the Department of Homeland Security's (DHS) budget request and about $14 million above the enacted fiscal year 2012 level.[7] The report noted that the funding was increased to ensure adequate resources to support potential new SPP participants and to encourage TSA to make greater use of the program. The report of the Committee on Appropriations of the Senate, however, recommended approximately $143 million for privatized screening for fiscal year 2013, the same amount requested in the budget and approximately $1 million below the enacted fiscal year 2012 level.[8] In its report, the Senate Committee explained that it expects TSA to not approve any new contract application for privatized screening if the annual cost of the contract exceeds the annual cost to TSA of providing federal screening services at that airport.

We reported in January 2009, among other things, that TSA had underestimated costs to the government for screeners at non-SPP airports because the agency did not include all of the costs associated with passenger and baggage screening services at these airports.[9] The omission of some cost factors reduced the reliability of TSA's 2009 cost estimate by increasing the costs for private-contractor screeners relative to federal screeners. We recommended that if TSA planned to rely on its comparison of cost and performance of SPP and non-SPP airports for future decision making, the agency should update its analysis to address

---

[6] See Pub. L. No. 112-95, § 830(a), 126 Stat. 11, 135 (2012) (codified at U.S.C. § 44920(b)).

[7] See H.R. Rpt. No. 112-492, at 64-65 (May 23, 2012) (accompanying H.R. 5855, 112th Cong. (2d Sess. 2012)).

[8] See S. Rpt. No. 112-169, at 60 (May 22, 2012) (accompanying S. 3216, 112th Cong. (2d Sess. 2012)).

[9] GAO, *Aviation Security: TSA's Cost and Performance Study of Private-Sector Airport Screening,* GAO-09-27R (Washington, D.C.: Jan. 9, 2009).

the limitations we identified. TSA generally concurred with our recommendation, and in March 2011, we reported that TSA has made progress in addressing the limitations related to costs and estimated that SPP airports would cost 3 percent more to operate in 2011 than airports using federal screeners.[10]

This report addresses the (1) status of airport applications made to the SPP, and airport operator, other stakeholders, and TSA views on the advantages and disadvantages of participating in the SPP; (2) extent to which TSA has provided guidance to govern the SPP application process; and (3) extent to which TSA assesses and monitors the performance of private and federal screeners.

This report is a public version of the prior sensitive report that we provided to you. DHS deemed some of the information in the prior report as Sensitive Security Information (SSI), which must be protected from public disclosure.[11] Therefore, this report omits information about the specific results of our comparison of SPP screener performance with performance of federal screeners across four performance measures we analyzed. Although the information provided in this report is more limited in scope, it addresses the same questions as the sensitive report. Also, the overall methodology used for both reports is the same.

To address all three of these objectives, we interviewed Federal Security Directors (FSD); airport operators; screeners; and where applicable, SPP contractors at 10 airports. We selected the 10 airports by matching an SPP to a non-SPP airport, in each of the five airport categories (category X, I, II, III, and IV), based primarily on (1) annual passenger and baggage volumes, (2) screener staffing model full-time equivalent allocation, and (3) number of check-points and screening lanes.[12] Additionally, on the basis of available travel resources, we visited 7 of the 10 airports to

---

[10]GAO, *Aviation Security: TSA'S Revised Cost Comparison Provides a More Reasonable Basis for Comparing the Costs of Private-Sector and TSA Screeners,* GAO-11-375R (Washington, D.C.: Mar. 4, 2011).

[11] See 49 C.F.R. pt. 1520.

[12]TSA classifies commercial airports in the United States into one of five security risk categories (X, I, II, III, and IV) based on various factors, such as the total number of takeoffs and landings annually, and other special security considerations. In general, category X airports have the largest number of passenger boardings, and category IV airports have the smallest.

observe airport screening operations, including any unique challenges faced by these airports. Our observations from these airport visits and interviews are illustrative and provide insights about private and federal screening operations but are not generalizable to all airports across the country.

To determine the status of SPP applications, and airport operators', other stakeholders', and TSA's views on the advantages and disadvantages of participating in the SPP, we interviewed officials of TSA's SPP Program Management Office (PMO) and reviewed the 15 SPP applications that had been submitted since fiscal year 2009, as well as TSA's available decision memos on the applications.[13] Further, we surveyed the 28 airport operators who have applied to the SPP since its inception through April 2012 (when the survey was implemented) to solicit their views on advantages and disadvantages for airports for participating in the SPP.[14] A 29th airport, Bozeman Yellowstone International Airport, applied to the SPP for the first time in June 2012 and, therefore, was not included in our survey. However, we interviewed this airport, as well as the 5 non-SPP airports we visited or interviewed, to obtain their perspectives on the potential advantages and disadvantages of participating in the SPP. We also interviewed representatives of three aviation industry associations to identify the advantages and disadvantages of using federal and nonfederal screeners.[15] We selected the three associations because they represent the majority of aviation industry stakeholders, including airport operators.

---

[13]TSA officials stated that decision memos were not available for all SPP applicants because, for example, they were not prepared or were lost when TSA transferred to a new file share program.

[14]The 28 airports whose airport operators we surveyed include 16 from airports that were participating in the SPP at the time of the survey, 2 airports that withdrew their applications before TSA made a decision, 3 airports that were approved but never transitioned to the SPP because commercial airline service was discontinued at the airport, and 7 airports that initially applied from March 2009 through April 2012 (when the survey was implemented).

[15]The three aviation industry associations we interviewed are International Air Transport Association, Airports Council International—North America, and the American Association of Airport Executives. Because we selected a nongeneralizable sample of aviation organizations, the information we gathered from our interviews with these organizations cannot be used to make inferences about all aviation organizations. However, we believe that the information we obtained was useful in learning about how such organizations view the SPP and their perspectives on how screener performance is assessed.

To determine the extent to which TSA has provided guidance to govern the SPP application process, we analyzed past and current SPP application forms and instructions, as well as interviewed TSA headquarters officials to identify the requirements and process for applying to the SPP. We surveyed operators of all approved SPP airports as well as operators of airports that have applied but are currently not participating in the SPP because TSA denied their application, or their participation is pending the procurement of a contractor, to determine their perspectives on the SPP application process. To determine if any improvements are needed to the SPP application process, we compared TSA's application process and requirements with *Standards for Internal Control in the Federal Government*.[16]

To determine the extent to which TSA assesses and monitors the performance of private and federal screeners, we interviewed TSA headquarters officials knowledgeable about TSA's performance management process to identify current screener performance measures. At the airports we visited, we observed screening operations to identify areas where screener performance could be assessed and interviewed contractor, airport, and TSA officials to obtain their perspectives on the current set of performance measures. We evaluated TSA's process for assessing and monitoring the performance of private and federal screeners against *Standards for Internal Control in the Federal Government* and best practices for performance management.[17] To determine how screener performance compares at SPP and non-SPP airports, we compared screener performance for the 16 currently participating SPP airports to the average performance of other airports in their category, as well as nationally, from fiscal year 2009 through 2011. To ensure the reliability of the performance measure data we analyzed, we (1) interviewed TSA officials who use and maintain the data; (2) checked the data for missing information, outliers, and obvious errors; and (3) reviewed documentation on the relevant data systems to ensure the data's integrity. On the basis of the steps we took, we found the data reliable for the purpose of providing summary statistics of screener

---

[16]GAO, *Standards for Internal Control in the Federal Government*, GAO/AIMD-00-21.3.1 (Washington, D.C.: November 1999).

[17]GAO/AIMD-00-21.3.1 and GAO, *Executive Guide: Effectively Implementing the Government Performance and Results Act*, GAO/GGD-96-118 (Washington, D.C.: June 1996); and *Tax Administration: IRS Needs to Further Refine Its Tax Filing Season Performance Measures*, GAO-03-143 (Washington, D.C.: November 2002).

performance for the four performance measures we analyzed. However, as we note later, because there are many factors that may account for differences in screener performance, some of which cannot be controlled for, any difference we found in screener performance at SPP and non-SPP airports cannot be entirely attributed to the use of either federal or private screeners.

We conducted this performance audit from November 2011 to November 2012, in accordance with generally accepted government auditing standards. Those standards require that we plan and perform the audit to obtain sufficient, appropriate evidence to provide a reasonable basis for our findings and conclusions based on our audit objectives. We believe that the evidence obtained provides a reasonable basis for our findings and conclusions based on our audit objectives. More details about the scope and methodology of our work are presented in appendix I.

Background

ATSA established TSA and charged it with responsibility for securing all modes of transportation, including civil aviation. Prior to ATSA and the establishment of TSA, passenger and baggage screening had generally been performed by private screening companies under contract to airlines and in accordance with FAA regulations. In accordance with ATSA, TSA currently employs personnel who screen passengers at the vast majority of TSA-regulated (also referred to as commercial) airports nationwide. On November 19, 2002, pursuant to ATSA, TSA began a 2-year pilot program at 5 airports using private screening companies to screen passengers and checked baggage.[18] In 2004, at the completion of the pilot program, and in accordance with ATSA, TSA established a permanent program known as the Screening Partnership Program whereby any airport authority, whether involved in the pilot or not, could request a transition from federal screeners to private, contracted screeners. Each of the 5 pilot airports applied and was approved to continue as part of the SPP, and since its establishment, 20 additional airport applications have been accepted by the SPP. Once an airport is

---

[18]See 49 U.S.C. § 44919. The pilot program was to assess the feasibility of having qualified private screening companies provide airport security screening services in lieu of federal screeners. The following airports from each security risk category were selected to participate: (1) San Francisco International Airport—category X, (2) Kansas City International Airport—category I, (3) Greater Rochester International Airport—category II (now a category I airport), (4) Jackson Hole Airport—category III, and (5) Tupelo Regional Airport—category IV.

approved for SPP participation and a private screening contractor has been selected, the contract screening workforce assumes responsibility for screening passengers and their property and must adhere to the same security regulations, standard operating procedures, and other TSA security requirements followed by federal screeners at commercial airports.

Federal and Private Screening Roles and Responsibilities

TSA's SPP PMO, located within TSA's Office of Security Operations (OSO), coordinates with local TSA officials to support an airport's transition from federal to private screening operations and supports the day-to-day management of the SPP. The PMO facilitates the SPP application process by reviewing SPP applications, organizing SPP application review meetings with other relevant TSA offices, and preparing and routing relevant application documentation to these offices and the TSA Administrator.[19] Along with the TSA Office of Acquisition, the office plays a significant role in contract oversight and administration, as well as actively participates in contract source selection processes.

TSA's FSDs provide day-to-day operational direction for security operations at the airports within their jurisdiction, including those participating in the SPP. However, FSD management responsibilities differ at airports using federal versus private screeners. For example, at airports with a federal workforce, the FSD directly supervises and controls the screening workforce. However, at SPP airports, the FSD has responsibility for overall security but does not have direct control over workforce management; rather the SPP contractor is contractually obligated to effectively and efficiently manage its screening workforce.

The SPP contractor's responsibilities include recruiting, assessing, and training screening personnel to provide security screening functions in accordance with TSA regulations, policies, and procedures. SPP contractors are also expected to take operational direction from TSA, through the FSDs, to help ensure they meet the terms and conditions of the contract. In addition, SPP contractors are rewarded for identifying and

---

[19]Relevant offices include, but are not limited to, the Office of Information Technology, the Office of Human Capital, and other TSA offices that affect airport operations and which together make up an Integrated Project Team (IPT) responsible for collecting, consolidating and reviewing SPP application data and preparing findings for the SPP Application Chair (SAC chair).

proposing ideas that TSA accepts for possible innovations in recruiting, training, and security procedures, such as the practice of conducting pre-hire orientations to inform prospective screener candidates of the position requirements, which is 1 of over 200 ideas submitted to TSA by SPP contractors to date.

Overview of the SPP Application Process

In March 2012, TSA revised the SPP application to reflect requirements of the FAA Modernization Act enacted in February 2012.[20] Among other provisions, the act provides that

- Not later than 120 days after the date of receipt of an SPP application submitted by an airport operator, the TSA Administrator must approve or deny the application.
- The TSA Administrator shall approve an application if approval would not (1) compromise security, (2) detrimentally affect the cost-efficiency of the screening of passengers or property at the airport, or (3) detrimentally affect the effectiveness of the screening of passengers or property at the airport.
- The airport operator shall include as part of its application submission a recommendation as to which private screening company would best serve the security screening and passenger needs of the airport.
- Within 60 days of a denial TSA must provide the airport operator, as well as the Committee on Commerce, Science, and Transportation of the Senate and the Committee on Homeland Security of the U.S. House of Representatives, a written report that sets forth the findings that served as the basis of the denial, the results of any cost or security analysis conducted in considering the application, and recommendations on how the airport operator can address the reasons for denial.

All commercial airports are eligible to apply to the SPP. To apply, an airport operator must complete the SPP application and submit it to the SPP PMO, as well as to the airport FSD, by mail, fax, or e-mail. As required by the FAA Modernization Act, not later than 120 days after the application is received by TSA, the Administrator must make a final decision on the application. Figure 1 illustrates the SPP application process.

---

[20] See generally Pub. L. No. 112-95, § 803, 126 Stat. at 135-36.

Figure 1: TSA's Screening Partnership Program (SPP) Application Process

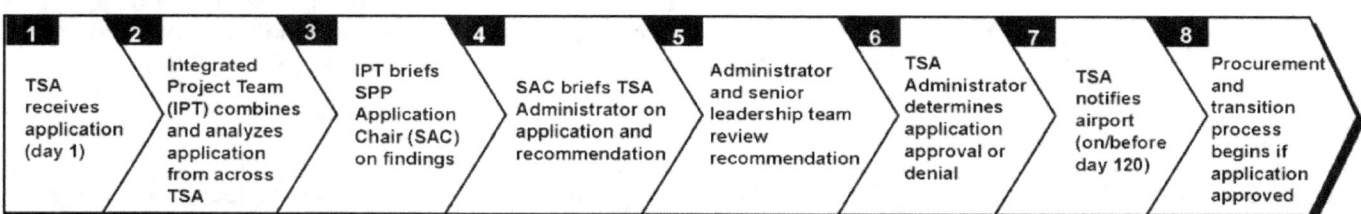

Source: GAO analysis of TSA information.

Note: The IPT is made up of TSA staff from various offices across TSA, including offices related to human capital, information technology, security capabilities, and acquisitions.

Although TSA provides all airports with the opportunity to apply for participation in the SPP, authority to approve or deny the application resides in the discretion of the TSA Administrator. According to TSA officials, in addition to the cost-efficiency and effectiveness considerations mandated by FAA Modernization Act, there are many other factors that are weighed in considering an airport's application for SPP participation. For example, the potential impact on the workload of the Office of Information Technology and the potential impact of any upcoming projects at the airport are considered. SPP PMO officials said that by considering all relevant factors, they do not expect to identify a specific piece of information that would definitively deny an application's approval based on the standards in the FAA Modernization Act. However, in doing so, they hope to ensure that the Administrator has the complete picture and could therefore make a decision using all factors in combination, consistent with the FAA Modernization Act. Nonetheless, factors found to be cost-prohibitive are likely to result in the airport being denied participation in the program.

TSA Implemented Prior Efforts Comparing Private and Federal Screening

In May 2007, TSA awarded a contract to Catapult Consultants to conduct a cost and performance analysis of airports with private screeners versus airports with federal screeners.[21] This analysis would be used to assist senior TSA leadership with strategic decisions regarding the degree to which TSA should leverage public/private partnerships in the area of screening services. According to the December 2007 report the

---

[21]TSA previously commissioned Bearing Point Consultants to conduct a similar study comparing the cost and performance of private and federal screeners, the results of which were published in 2004.

contractor issued on its analysis, SPP airports performed at a level equal to or better than non-SPP airports for the four performance measures included in the analysis.[22] Following this study, in February 2008, TSA issued a report on a study TSA conducted comparing the cost and performance of screening at SPP and non-SPP airports.[23] The study compared performance measures at each of six SPP airports to the non-SPP airports in the same airport category and found that SPP airports generally performed consistently with non-SPP airports in their category for the performance measures included in its analysis.[24]

---

[22]Catapult Consultants, LLC, *Private Screening Operations: Business Case Analysis, Transportation Security Administration, Screening Partnership Program* (Arlington: VA: Dec.14, 2007). The performance measures used in this analysis were threat image projection (TIP) detection rate, recertification pass rate, wait time, and the results of a TSA sponsored customer satisfaction survey. We describe TIP detection rates and recertification pass rate later in this report.

[23]Transportation Security Administration, *A Report on SPP Airport Cost and Performance Analysis and Comparison to Business Case Analysis Finding* (Arlington, VA: Feb. 1, 2008).

[24]In conducting the study, TSA compared the cost of operating screening at the six SPP airports in its study with the cost that would be incurred in the agency's budget if these airports were run as fully federal or non-SPP airports. TSA found that screening at SPP airports at the time cost approximately 17.4 percent more to operate than at airports with federal screeners. In its report, TSA considered an airport to be an "average" performer if the results of the performance measure fell within one standard deviation from the airport category average (the middle 68.2 percent of the category). On the basis of results for the six airports it included in its analysis, TSA found that the majority of the SPP airports fell within the average performer category for the five performance measures it included in its analysis. The measures TSA used in its study were TIP detection rates; screener recertification pass rates; the percentage of passengers that experienced a wait time under 10 minutes; the length of time of the peak wait time; and the checkpoint capacity utilization rate, which is the average of the percentage of lanes utilized and the percentage of throughput compared with full capacity.

TSA Has Approved 25 SPP Applications; Enhanced Customer Service Was the Most Commonly Cited Advantage of the SPP

SPP Applicants and Participating Airports

Since the inception of the SPP in 2004, 29 airports have applied for participation in the program; 25 airports have been approved, and as we noted earlier in this report, 16 airports are participating in the SPP as of October 2012.[25] A detailed timeline and status of each airport application are provided in figure 2 and appendix II.

---

[25] Four of the 29 airports applied to the SPP more than once because TSA either denied their initial application or requested that they re-submit their application using a revised SPP application form. The 5 airports participating in the pilot program were required to submit applications to continue private screening operations under the SPP.

Figure 2: Screening Partnership Program (SPP) Application History

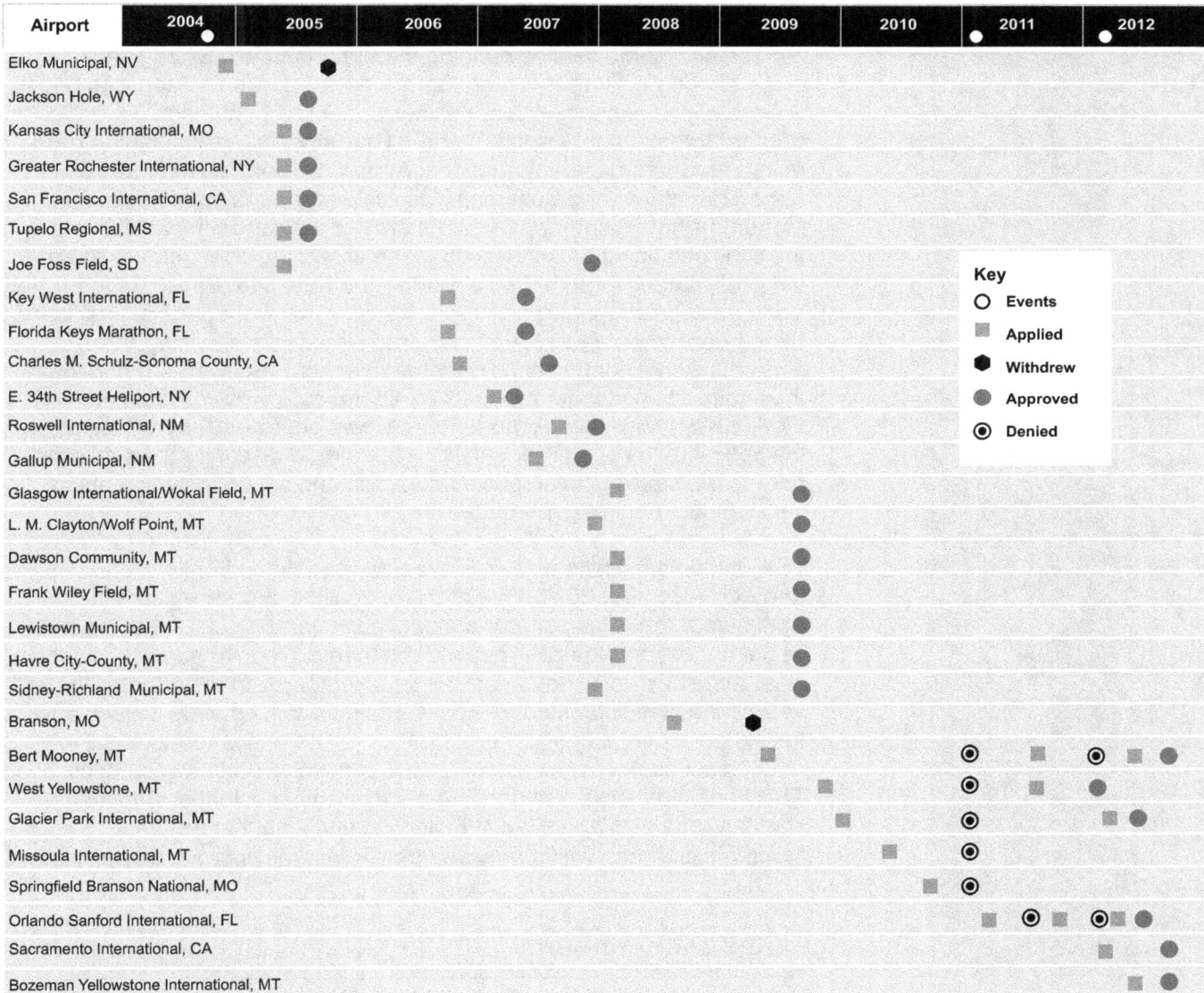

Source: GAO analysis of TSA information.

Note: Sacramento International Airport submitted its first application to the SPP approximately 1 week before the FAA Modernization and Reform Act of 2012 was enacted. In March 2012, TSA revised the SPP application to facilitate compliance with provisions of the act and requested that Sacramento International Airport resubmit its application using the new application form. While the airport submitted its new application form in April 2012, TSA considers the date of receipt to still be February 2012.

GAO-13-208 Screening Partnership Program

Nine airports were approved but are not currently participating in the program because they are either (1) in the process of having an SPP contractor procured, (2) were once part of the SPP but ceased screening services when commercial airline service placing the airport under TSA regulation was discontinued, or (3) never transitioned to the SPP because commercial airline service bringing the airport under TSA regulation to these airports was discontinued before private screening services began. Specifically, 6 airports—West Yellowstone Airport, Montana; Orlando Sanford International Airport, Florida; Glacier Park International Airport, Montana; Sacramento International Airport, California; Bert Mooney Airport, Montana; and Bozeman Yellowstone International Airport, Montana—have been approved but are not yet currently participating in the SPP pending TSA's selection of the screening contractor to provide services at each airport. Two airports—the East 34th Street Heliport, New York, and Gallup Municipal Airport, New Mexico were participating in the SPP, but according to TSA officials, the air carriers servicing these airports discontinued service after the contract was awarded, and thus these airports no longer required TSA screening services. Additionally, Florida Keys Marathon Airport, Florida, was approved for participation in the SPP, but the air carrier servicing the airport discontinued services prior to the start of the screening contract, and accordingly screening services were no longer required.

TSA denied applications from 6 airports—submitted from March 2009 through December 2011. Five of these applications were submitted to TSA before the Administrator announced in January 2011 that the agency would not expand the SPP beyond the then current 16 airports "unless a clear and substantial advantage to do so emerges in the future." The sixth application was submitted for consideration approximately 1 week after the Administrator's announcement. Prior to the enactment of the FAA Modernization Act in February 2012, 1 of the 6 airports whose application TSA denied re-applied under TSA's "clear and substantial advantage" standard and was approved.[26] Following enactment of the FAA Modernization Act, which provided that TSA shall approve an application

---

[26]According to TSA officials, TSA's decision to approve the 1 airport that reapplied under the agency's "clear and substantial advantage" standard was based on a more detailed cost analysis the agency conducted that showed that because of the airport's reliance on TSA's National Deployment Force, it would indeed be cheaper for a screening contractor to provide screening services at this airport. The National Deployment Force is composed of a team of federal screeners who assist when there are event or crisis-related situations that require additional security-related screening support.

if approval would not compromise security or detrimentally affect the cost-efficiency or the effectiveness of the screening of passengers or property at the airport, TSA approved the applications of 3 other airports who reapplied. Two of the 6 airports that had been denied never reapplied for participation in the SPP (see fig. 2 for additional details). Figure 3 and appendix III show the locations of the 16 airports currently participating in the SPP as well as the 6 airports that TSA recently approved for participation.

Figure 3: Airports Participating in or Recently Approved for Participation in the Screening Partnership Program (SPP)

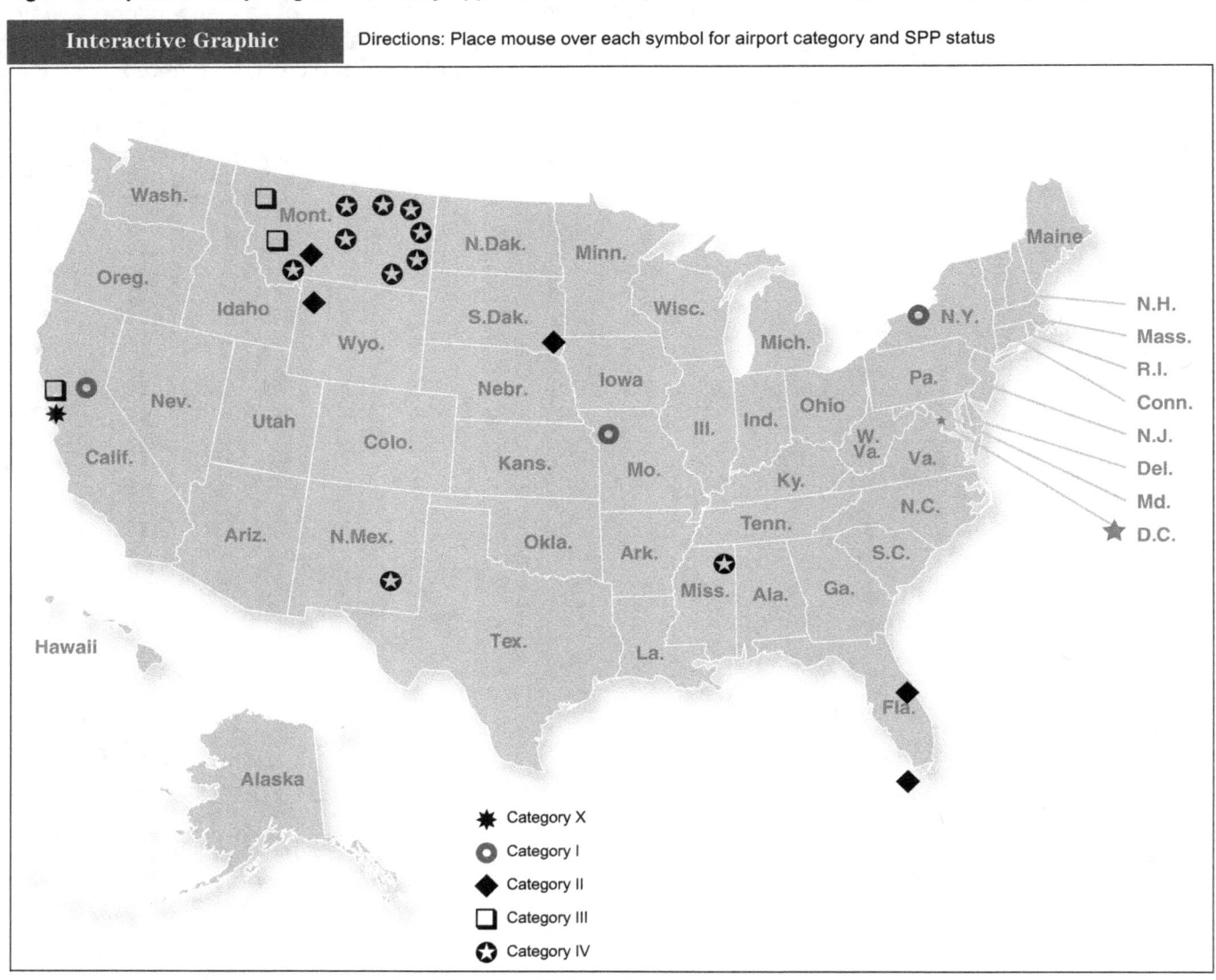

Source: GAO analysis of TSA information.

Note; TSA classifies commercial airports in the United States into one of five security risk categories (X, I, II, III, and IV) based on various factors, such as the total number of takeoffs and landings annually, and other special security considerations. In general, category X airports have the largest number of passenger boardings, and category IV airports have the smallest

As figure 3 shows, 10 of 16 of the airports currently participating in the SPP are smaller, category III and IV airports, with 9 of those located in the western region of the United States.

In recent years, the number of airports applying for participation in the SPP has generally declined. Specifically, from 2004 through 2008, 21 airports applied to the SPP, including the 5 airports that participated in TSA's SPP pilot program. Since 2009, TSA has received SPP applications from 8 airports.

Reported Advantages and Disadvantages of Joining the SPP

Airport operators we surveyed and interviewed, as well as aviation industry stakeholders (i.e., aviation associations) and TSA officials we interviewed, most commonly cited customer service and staffing flexibility as advantages of participating in the SPP, but also expressed concerns about the SPP transition process and satisfaction with existing TSA screening services as potential disadvantages of participating in the program.[27] We surveyed 28 airport operators who had applied to the SPP from its inception in 2004 through April 2012. Twenty-six operators responded. Because all 26 survey respondents were airport operators who have applied to the SPP, these airport operators may be more likely to present positive views of, or what they perceived of, the SPP. In addition, perspectives may also be influenced by whether or not the operators were approved for participation in the SPP at the time the survey was conducted. We also interviewed 6 airport operators that were not included in our survey. Five of these airport operators have not applied for participation in the SPP, and 1 airport operator had applied for participation after our survey was conducted, and therefore was not included as part of our survey.

Our 2012 survey and interviews of airport operators include the following highlights:

Advantages to SPP

The advantages most frequently identified by the airport operators that had applied to the SPP and responded to our survey and those we interviewed (including those that had not applied to the SPP) were related

---

[27]Similarly, in 2009 we reported that airport operators we interviewed cited customer service and the ability to alleviate TSA staffing concerns as a reason for deciding to participate in the SPP, and satisfaction with TSA's screening workforce as the primary disadvantage of participating in the SPP. See GAO-09-27R.

to providing better customer service and obtaining flexibility assigning staff. The airport associations most commonly cited obtaining flexibility in assigning staff as an advantage. Because TSA generally remains neutral regarding the SPP, the views of TSA officials expressed are attributed to the individual FSDs we interviewed and do not reflect the views of the agency.

- **Customer service.** Sixteen airport operators we surveyed and interviewed reported customer service as an advantage—15 had applied to the SPP and 1 had not.[28] Specifically, 14 of 26 airport operators responding to the survey indicated this was a realized or potential advantage to a great or very great extent.[29] In addition, 2 of the 6 airport operators we interviewed, 1 of which applied to the SPP, stated that the level of customer service provided by security screeners is particularly important for smaller community-based airports. These airports constitute the majority of the airports participating in the SPP, because passengers who have negative encounters with the screening process generally associate their experiences with the specific airport. Thus, airport officials stated that this might increase the likelihood that the passengers involved will seek alternative modes of transportation or different airports for future travel. Representatives from the three airport associations we interviewed did not identify customer service as an advantage of the SPP. TSA officials stated that federal screeners can and do provide similar levels of customer service and that most commercial airports are content to have a TSA workforce at their airports. TSA also stated that customer service is an important aspect of their work, and that the agency is taking steps to improve customer service in a way that does not jeopardize the agency's core mission, which is to ensure the security of the traveling public. Specifically, TSA officials said that they have enhanced their performance management processes to

---

[28]We surveyed and interviewed a total of 32 airport operators regarding the advantages and disadvantages of participating in the SPP.

[29]Our survey population included 28 airports that have applied for participation in the SPP. Of these 28, 26 airports responded to the survey. Survey respondents were asked to rate the extent to which various factors presented in the survey were an advantage, or disadvantage, of participating in the SPP. We use the terms "great extent" and "very great extent" to determine the extent to which airport operators identified a primary advantage or disadvantage of participating in the SPP.

better gauge customer service, such as tracking negative contacts received at airports.

- **Staffing flexibility.** Fifteen airport operators we surveyed and interviewed—14 had applied to the SPP and 1 had not—and representatives from two aviation industry associations reported that private screening contractors are generally more responsive and flexible than TSA to increasing staffing needs in response to fluctuations in passenger volume at the airport. Specifically, 13 of 26 airport operators responding to our survey cited flexibility in assigning staff as a realized or potential advantage to a great or very great extent of participating in the SPP. Two of the 6 airport operators we interviewed, 1 of which had applied to the SPP, also cited staffing flexibility as an advantage. For example, an airport operator highlighted challenges the airport has faced in adjusting the number of screening staff to accommodate the seasonal changes in passenger volume at his airport. Specifically, the airport operator, a current SPP participant, commented that unlike TSA screeners, private screening contractors are able to staff screeners in split shifts—a work period divided into two or more periods of time, such as morning and evening, with a break of several hours between—thereby enabling them to adjust to the airport's flight schedule and changes in passenger volume.[30] TSA officials disagreed with this view and stated that TSA provides FSDs with discretion to utilize federal screeners in split shifts during the course of the workday, provided that such discretion is exercised as the direct result of operational need. Furthermore, TSA officials stated that all category IV and many category III airports use split shifts. Four of six FSDs we interviewed cited a reduced involvement in human resource management as an advantage to the federal government for participating in the SPP. For example, one FSD said that because TSA oversees the screening operations of SPP airports and FSDs are not involved with deploying and managing screening staff, they are better able to focus on their security oversight functions, including ensuring that proper standard operating procedures are being followed.

---

[30]According to TSA, split shifts are likely to be used at smaller airports which generally have fewer and less frequent flights a day, and consequently experience significant fluctuations in passenger volume.

- **Cost savings.** During our follow-up interviews with survey respondents, 4 airport operators said that participating in the SPP could help alleviate TSA resource constraints and result in cost savings to the federal government because some airports that are currently participating in or applied for participation in the SPP are located in certain rural or high-cost communities where the federal government has difficulty hiring screeners and must utilize federal personnel deployed for temporary assignments, which results in increased costs. An FSD of an SPP airport located in a small, high-cost community we interviewed agreed that the salary offered by TSA made it difficult to fill screening positions at the airport, stating that prior to the airport's transition to the SPP, TSA had difficulty hiring screeners from the local area, and as a result had to use screeners from its National Deployment Force (NDF), a deployable federal screening workforce, because of the high cost of living in the area.[31] To maintain the requisite level of screening services at airports in environments where it is hard to recruit, TSA often uses screeners from its NDF, which TSA stated can be more expensive than SPP screeners because the NDF screeners are compensated on a per diem basis when deployed and incur other costs such as temporary housing expenses.

Disadvantages

Airport operators generally cited few realized or potential disadvantages of participating in the SPP. Six airport operators we surveyed and interviewed cited the discontinuation of federal screening services as a potential disadvantage of participating in the SPP. Specifically, the 4 of 25 survey respondents who had applied to the SPP program cited the discontinuation of federal screening services as a potential disadvantage of participating in the SPP.[32] In addition, 2 airport operators who have not applied to the SPP expressed concerns about the potential disruption

---

[31]According to this airport official, private screening contractors may be able to offer higher wages to make screening positions more competitive in environments where it is otherwise hard to recruit. In accordance with 49 U.S.C. § 44920(d), screening contractors must provide compensation and other benefits at a level not less than the compensation and other benefits provided to TSA screeners, but are not prohibited from offering compensation and benefits at a higher level.

[32]All 26 survey respondents applied to the SPP. We use the terms "great extent" and "very great extent" to determine the extent to which airport operators identified a primary advantage or disadvantage of participating in the SPP. One survey respondent did not provide a response to this question, therefore the total number of respondents for this question is 25.

associated with the transition from TSA screeners to private screeners at their airports, and the associated risk of doing so if the process does not proceed as smoothly as intended.[33] One of these airport operators stated that concerns about the transition process—going from federal screeners to private screeners—is the primary reason the airport has not submitted an application. Further, this airport operator also cited concerns about maintaining screener morale, and hence security, as a major reason for the airport's decision to not apply to the SPP.[34] Officials from the aviation industry associations we interviewed did not cite any realized or potential disadvantages. As noted earlier, TSA generally remains neutral regarding the SPP, and accordingly did not cite disadvantages of participating in the SPP.

Additionally, airport operators from 3 airports that have not applied to the SPP expressed no interest in the SPP, and stated that they are generally satisfied with the level of screening service provided by TSA. Similarly, an Airport Council International-North America (ACI-NA) March 2007 study found that 71 percent of 31 survey respondents were not interested in the SPP, and cited satisfaction with TSA screening services, among other things, for not having any interest in the SPP.[35] When asked, representatives from all three aviation industry associations we interviewed either expressed no opinion on the SPP or cited no disadvantages to participating in the SPP. Two of these industry representatives added that the majority of the airports they represent are generally satisfied with the screening services provided by TSA.

---

[33]As part of our review, we obtained perspectives from airport operators who have not applied for participation to the SPP.

[34]The remaining airport operators cited disadvantages; however, there were no common themes among the disadvantages cited with the exceptions of those identified disadvantages noted above.

[35]Airports Council International-North America, *Screening Partnership Program: Interest and Considerations*, March 12, 2007. ACI-NA received a total of 31 survey responses. Because of the low response rate to the survey, the views reported in the survey reflect the views of the 31 who responded to the survey and not necessarily the views of the membership as a whole.

TSA Has Developed Application Resources, but Could Provide Guidance for SPP Applicants

TSA has developed some resources to assist applicants; however, it has not provided guidance on its application and approval process to assist airports with applying to the program. As the application process was originally implemented, TSA required that an airport operator interested in applying to the program submit an application stating its intention to opt out of federal screening as well as its reason(s) for wanting to do so. However, in 2011, TSA revised its SPP application to reflect the "clear and substantial advantage" standard announced by the Administrator in January 2011. Specifically, TSA requested that the applicant explain how private screening at the airport would provide a clear and substantial advantage to TSA's security operations.[36] At the time, TSA did not provide written guidance to airports to assist them in understanding what would constitute a "clear and substantial advantage to TSA security operations" or TSA's basis for determining whether an airport had established that opting out would present a clear and substantial advantage to TSA security operations. TSA officials told us that they did not issue guidance at the time in conjunction with the new standard because the agency desired to maintain a neutral position on the SPP and did not want to influence an airport's decision to participate in the program. In the absence of such guidance, SPP officials told us that they were available to provide assistance, if requested, to airports that sought assistance or information on completing their application.

In March 2012, TSA again revised the SPP application in accordance with provisions of the FAA Modernization Act enacted in February 2012. Among other things, the revised application no longer includes the "clear and substantial advantage" question, but instead includes questions that request applicants to discuss how participating in the SPP would not compromise security at the airport and to identify potential areas where

---

[36]The question in the application stated: "TSA has determined that the best way to maximize its effectiveness as a Federal counterterrorism security agency is to expand the Screening Partnership Program only where there would be a clear and substantial advantage to do so. However, the Agency is open to new and innovative ideas and opportunities to manage TSA's operations more efficiently, while maintaining our high standards and meeting the threats of today and the future. Please explain how private screening at your airport would provide a clear and substantial advantage to TSA's security operations (attach all supporting documentation)."

cost savings or efficiencies may be realized.[37] Additionally, in accordance with the FAA Modernization Act, applicants must recommend a contractor that would best serve the security screening and passenger needs of the airport. TSA officials told us that the agency offers potential applicants numerous points of contact and methods with which the applicants can discuss the program before applying to participate. Specifically, applicants can discuss the program with their FSD, the SPP program manager, or their recommended screening contractor. Further, according to TSA officials, once an airport operator submits an application, TSA assigns a program official as a point of contact for the application, and works with the applicant to ensure the application is complete and to keep the applicant informed. TSA also provides general instructions for filling out the SPP application as well as responses to frequently asked questions (FAQ). However, TSA has not issued guidance to assist airports with completing the new application and has not explained to airports how it will evaluate applications given the changes brought about by the new law. Neither the current application instructions nor the FAQs address TSA's SPP application evaluation process or its basis for determining whether an airport's entry into SPP would compromise security or affect cost-efficiency and effectiveness.

We interviewed 4 of the 5 airport operators that applied to the SPP since TSA revised its application in the wake of the FAA Modernization Act. Three of the 5 told us that they struggled to answer the application questions related to the cost-efficiency of converting to the SPP because they did not have data on federal screening costs, while the fourth airport operator said that she did not need additional information or guidance to respond to the question. One of the 4 airport operators stated that he needed the cost information to help demonstrate that his airport's participation in the SPP would not detrimentally affect the cost-efficiency of the screening of passengers or property at the airport and that he believes not presenting this information would be detrimental to his airport's application. However, TSA officials said that the cost information

---

[37]The questions relate to a provision of the FAA Modernization Act stating that the TSA Administrator "shall approve an application submitted by an airport operator if the Administrator determines that the approval would not compromise security or detrimentally affect the cost-efficiency or the effectiveness of the screening of passengers or property at the airport." See 49 U.S.C. § 44920(b)(2). Although responses to these questions are optional, some SPP applicants reported that because the questions relate to specific provisions in the law, they thought not responding to the questions would be detrimental to their applications.

required to answer the questions is basic cost information that airports should already maintain and that airports do not need to provide this information to TSA because, as part of the application evaluation process, TSA conducts a more detailed cost analysis using historical cost data from SPP and non-SPP airports. TSA officials added that the SPP application and the cost information requested only serve to alert TSA of things it may not be already aware of about the airport. The absence of cost and other information in an individual airport's application, TSA officials noted, would not materially affect the TSA Administrator's decision on an SPP application.

Three of the 4 airport operators we interviewed, and whose applications TSA subsequently approved after enactment of the FAA Modernization Act, said that additional guidance would have been helpful in completing the application and determining how TSA evaluates the applications. A representative from 1 of the 3 airports stated that while TSA officials have been more responsive and accessible since enactment of the FAA Modernization Act, the agency has not necessarily been helpful with the application process. Moreover, all 4 airport operators we interviewed told us that TSA did not specifically assign a point of contact when they applied to the program. Rather, all 4 airport operators reported consulting the SPP PMO, their FSD, or their recommended contractor because they needed information on such issues as screening cost, the list of current SPP contractors, TSA screener staffing levels, and examples of additional information they should provide TSA because they could not answer some of the application questions without this information. Specifically, 1 of the 4 airport operators reported contacting the FSD to request assistance with completing the application, while 2 of the four said they did not because FSDs generally are not knowledgeable about the program or are able to provide only general as opposed to detailed information about the application process. Instead of contacting their FSDs, these 2 airport operators told us that they contacted the SPP PMO and stated that the office were helpful in providing general information, such as a list of current SPP contractors, but not screening cost or other specific application information that would help the airports demonstrate whether the use of private screeners would compromise security or detrimentally affect the cost-efficiency or effectiveness of the screening of passengers or property at the airport. Another airport operator who reported contacting the SPP PMO stated that she learned about TSA's SPP selection criteria and processes in the course of her discussions with one of the SPP managers with whom she had developed a working relationship over the years, and added that had she not contacted this particular manager, she would not have obtained this information because TSA does not publish the information for other airports that may be interested in obtaining the information. Three of the 4 airport operators who told us they sought information to complete their application from their recommended contractor as advised by TSA stated that the contractors told them they did not have the necessary cost information to assist the airports with responding to the application questions related to the cost-efficiency of converting to the SPP.

Following enactment of the FAA Modernization Act, TSA officials initially stated that application guidance is not needed because the "clear and substantial" basis for joining the SPP has been eliminated and responses to the two new application questions related to cost-efficiency and effectiveness are optional responses. However, the Assistant Administrator for the Office of Security Operations now agrees that providing additional high-level guidance on the kind of information TSA considers during the application review phase would be helpful to SPP applicants. TSA SPP officials also stated that they routinely talk about the SPP at industry briefings and that they have done a good job of explaining the new application to industry. However, as of September 2012, representatives of all three aviation industry associations we interviewed told us that TSA has not provided any information on the SPP to their association since enactment of the FAA Modernization Act in February 2012. Additionally, representatives of two of the three aviation industry associations said that providing guidance or information on the criteria TSA uses to evaluate applications would be helpful to their members, while a representative from the third aviation association that represents domestic and international airline carriers said that its members would appreciate any basic information on the SPP. In interviews we conducted prior to the enactment of the FAA Modernization Act, these same aviation industry representatives told us that the absence of guidance provided by TSA is a barrier to applying to the program. They added that most airports do not want to invest in preparing an application when they are unsure as to how it would be evaluated by TSA.

TSA has approved all applications submitted since enactment of the FAA Modernization Act; however, it is hard to determine how many more airports, if any, would have applied to the program had TSA provided application guidance and information to improve transparency of the SPP application process. In the absence of such application guidance and information, it will be difficult for more airport officials to evaluate whether their airports are good candidates for the SPP or determine what criteria TSA uses to accept and approve airports' SPP applications. Further, airports may be missing opportunities to provide TSA with cost and other information that TSA would find useful in reviewing airport applications. According to *Standards for Internal Control in the Federal Government*, internal control and all transactions and other significant events need to be clearly documented, and the documentation should be readily available for examination.[38] The documentation should appear in management directives, administrative policies, or operating manuals and may be in paper or electronic form. Clear guidance for applying to the SPP could improve the transparency of the SPP application process and help ensure that the existing application process is implemented in a consistent and uniform manner.

TSA Has Measures to Assess Screener Performance, but Enhanced Processes for Evaluating Screener Performance Could Be Beneficial

TSA improved its set of screener performance measures in 2012 by adding measures that address passenger satisfaction, thereby ensuring that the measures address all aspects of the agency's airport screening strategic goals and mission. However, a mechanism to monitor private versus federal screener performance could help TSA to routinely ensure that the level of screening services and protection provided at SPP airports continues to be conducted at acceptable levels provided at non-SPP airports, and could help inform TSA managers when making decisions regarding the future of the SPP, such as whether to expand the program to more non-SPP airports. While we found differences in screener performance between SPP and non-SPP airports, those differences cannot be entirely attributed to the use of either private or federal screeners.

Performance between SPP and Non-SPP Airports Varies for Some Measures, but Differences Cannot Be Entirely Attributed to the Use of Private or Federal Screeners

We analyzed screener performance data for four measures and found that while there are differences in performance between SPP and non-SPP airports, those differences cannot be exclusively attributed to the use of either federal or private screeners. We selected these measures primarily based on our review of previous studies that compared screener performance of SPP and non-SPP airports as well as on our interviews with aviation security subject matter experts, including TSA's FSDs, SPP contractors, and airport and aviation industry stakeholders. We also selected performance measures for which TSA has, for the most part, consistently and systematically collected data from fiscal year 2009

---

[38]GAO/AIMD-00-21.3.1

through 2011.[39] The measures we selected to compare screener performance at SPP and non-SPP airports are TIP detection rates, recertification pass rates, Aviation Security Assessment Program (ASAP) test results, and Presence, Advisement, Communication, and Execution (PACE) evaluation results (see table 1). For each of these four measures, we compared the performance of each of the 16 SPP airports with the average performance for each airport's category (X, I, II, III, or IV), as well as the national performance averages for all airports for fiscal years 2009 through 2011.

Table 1: Performance Measures GAO Used to Compare Screener Performance at SPP and Non-SPP airports

Performance measure	Description
TIP detection rates	TIPs are fictional threat images (guns, knives, improvised explosive devices, etc.) superimposed onto carry-on baggage as it passes through the X-ray machine. While screening carry-on baggage, screeners identify that a potential threat has been spotted by selecting a "threat" button. If the identified image is a TIP, the X-ray machine informs the screener that the threat was fictional. Otherwise, a screener will search the bag, as the threat object may be real. The TIP detection rate is the number of TIPs correctly identified by screeners divided by the total number of TIPs that were presented.
Recertification pass rates	In order to maintain their certification to screen passengers and baggage, all screeners (at both SPP and non-SPP airports) must pass several recertification tests on an annual basis.[a] These tests include assessments of threat detection skills on carry-on and checked baggage X-ray machines as well as role-playing scenarios to assess other job functions, such as physical bag searches, pat downs, and screening passengers with disabilities. The recertification pass rate is the total number of required tests passed on the first attempt divided by the total number of tests taken at a given airport.
ASAP tests results	ASAP tests are covert performance assessments conducted at both screening checkpoints and checked baggage screening areas. Tests are implemented locally by unrecognizable role players who attempt to pass standard test items, such as knives, guns, or simulated improvised explosive devices, through the screening checkpoints or checked baggage screening areas. ASAP tests are designed to determine screener compliance with screening standard operating procedures. Unlike covert "red team" tests that are used to identify system-wide vulnerabilities, ASAP tests are designed to determine screener compliance with screening standard operating procedures. TSA began standardizing ASAP tests in fiscal year 2011 such that airports are required to take the same tests instead of picking their own tests.[b] The ASAP test pass rate is the number of tests passed divided by the total number of tests taken.

---

[39]Some of the measures we selected, such as PACE evaluation data, were not available for all 3 years or all airports; nonetheless, we selected these measures because they represent integral aspects of screener performance.

GAO-13-208 Screening Partnership Program

Performance measure	Description
PACE evaluations	PACE evaluations, which began in fiscal year 2011, are used to assess screener performance on various elements that may affect security and a passenger's overall travelling experience. Specifically, the evaluations assess the level of standardization across airports in the following four areas: presence (i.e., command presence), advisement (i.e., telling passengers what to do), communication, and execution. PACE evaluators visit a checkpoint covertly and assess the screening personnel on a variety of elements, such as whether the officers provide comprehensive instruction and engage passengers in a calm and respectful manner when screening. Because PACE evaluations began as a baseline assessment program in fiscal year 2011 and have only been implemented at category X, I, and II airports, our analysis for this measure was limited to the 6 SPP airports in those categories during fiscal year 2011.[c]

Source: GAO analysis of TSA information.

Notes: ASAP tests and PACE evaluations have not been used in the past to compare private and federal screener performance, but TSA officials noted that they would consider using them in the future.

[a]Federal and private screeners take initial certification tests after they are hired and do not take recertification tests until the next annual performance cycle.

[b]In addition to ASAP tests, TSA's Office of Inspections also conducts covert tests, commonly referred to as "red team tests" that are designed to assess TSA's screening operations for potential vulnerabilities.

[c]The six category X, I, and II SPP airports in fiscal year 2011 are San Francisco International Airport (X), Kansas City International Airport (I), Greater Rochester International Airport (I), Key West International Airport (II), Joe Foss Field (II), and Jackson Hole Airport (II).

On the basis of our analyses, we found that, generally, certain SPP airports performed slightly above the airport category and national averages for some measures, while others performed slightly below. For example, SPP airports performed above their respective airport category averages for recertification pass rates in the majority of instances, while the majority of SPP airports that took PACE evaluations in 2011 performed below their airport category averages on their PACE evaluations.[40] For TIP detection rates, SPP airports performed above their respective airport category averages in about half of the instances. DHS deemed the details of our analyses of the four performance measures we used for comparing SPP with non-SPP screener performance as classified or sensitive security information; thus, these details are not included in this report.[41]

---

[40] For recertification pass rates, the term "instance" means performance by an airport during a particular year or fiscal year while for TIP detection rates, the term means performance by an airport during a particular fiscal year for a specific type of screening machine.

[41] Details of our analyses of recertification pass rates, PACE evaluations, and TIP detection rates can be found in the sensitive security version of this report; however, ASAP test results were omitted from that report because ASAP results are classified.

The differences we observed in private and federal screener performance cannot be entirely attributed to the type of screeners (private or federal) at an airport, because, according to TSA officials and other subject matter experts we interviewed, many factors, some of which cannot be controlled for, affect screener performance. These factors include, but are not limited to, checkpoint layout, airline schedules, seasonal changes in travel volume, and type of traveler. For example, TSA officials told us that the type of traveler experienced by an airport can affect the average wait time at an airport. Airports located in areas near tourist locations, for example, may experience higher volumes of first-time and infrequent travelers, as opposed to business travelers that fly more frequently. Infrequent travelers are more likely to bring prohibited items through the checkpoint because they are unfamiliar with TSA's security protocols, a fact that can result in more bags needing to be searched and, consequently, longer wait times. Accordingly, while there may be differences in performance between an airport near a tourist location and an airport not located near a tourist location, those differences may be attributed to the type of passenger and not the use of either federal or private screeners at these airports. However, while differences in performance cannot be entirely attributed to the type of screener, differences and changes over time may still be of interest to TSA managers and may inform decision making regarding the future use of private contractor screeners, which we discuss later.

TSA collects data on several other performance measures but, for various reasons, they cannot be used to compare private and federal screener performance for the purposes of our review. For example, we do not present passenger wait time data because we found that TSA's policy for collecting wait times changed during the time period of our analyses and that these data were not collected in a consistent manner across all airports. We also considered reviewing human capital measures such as attrition, absenteeism, and injury rates, but did not analyze these data because TSA's Office of Human Capital does not collect these data for SPP airports. While the contractors collect and report this information to TSA, TSA does not validate the accuracy of the self-reported data nor does it require contractors to use the same human capital measures as TSA, and accordingly, differences may exist in how the metrics are defined and how the data are collected. Therefore, TSA cannot guarantee that a comparison of SPP and non-SPP airports on these human capital metrics would be an equal comparison. In appendix IV, we discuss these two variables as well as two other variables occasionally cited by the airport officials and aviation stakeholders we interviewed as possible measures for comparing federal and private screening and the reasons we did not use them to compare private and federal screener performance.

TSA Recently Improved Its Screener Performance Measures to Ensure the Measures Address Strategic Goals and Mission

Beginning in April 2012, TSA introduced a new set of performance measures to assess screener performance at both SPP and non-SPP airports in its OSO Executive Scorecard (Scorecard). OSO officials told us that they provide the Scorecard to FSDs every 2 weeks to assist the FSDs with tracking performance against stated goals and with determining how performance of the airports under their jurisdiction compares with national averages. According to TSA, the 10 measures now used in the Scorecard were selected based on input from FSDs and regional directors on the performance measures that most adequately reflect screener and airport performance. Prior to the Scorecard, from 2006 through April 2012, FSDs used three performance measures in the Management Objective Report (MOR) to assess screener and airport performance (see table 2). Further, TSA improved upon the set of measures it uses to assess screener performance by adding measures to the Scorecard that addressed other non-security-related TSA priorities, such as passenger satisfaction. Specifically, the Scorecard includes passenger satisfaction measures, such as the number of negative and positive customer contacts made to the TSA Contact Center through e-mails or phone calls per 100,000 passengers screened through the airport, which were not previously included in the MOR.[42] By adding measures related to passenger satisfaction to the Scorecard, TSA helped to ensure balance—that is, addressing a variety of agency goals—in the set of performance measures the agency uses to assess screener performance, which helps to ensure that performance measurement efforts are not overemphasizing one or two priorities at the expense of others. Details on our assessment of the MOR and Scorecard are provided in appendix V. While many of the measures used to assess screener performance are included in the Scorecard, several are not, but are available to TSA officials through other reports and databases. For example, TSA officials are able to review reports on their passenger throughput, wait times, and covert test results—information that is not included in the Scorecard.

---

[42]The TSA Contact Center handles these customer contacts for all of TSA, not only those related to passenger and baggage screening. The passenger satisfaction metrics in the Scorecard do not include other types of customer contacts made by passengers, such as via comment cards at local airports or letters written to the TSA Administrator.

Table 2: Management Objective Report and Scorecard Performance Measures

MOR performance measures	Scorecard performance measures
TIP detection rate	TIP detection rate
Advanced Imaging Technology (AIT) checkpoint utilization[a]	Percentage of passengers screened with an AIT machine
Layered security effectiveness[b]	Selectee miss rate[c]
	Recertification pass rate[d]
	Number of checkpoint closures less than 10 minutes
	Number of checkpoint closures greater than 10 minutes
	Negative customer contacts per 100,000 customers
	Positive customer contacts per 100,000 customers
	Percentage of passengers waiting between 20 and 30 minutes
	Percentage of passengers waiting greater than 30 minutes

Source: GAO analysis of TSA information.

Note: Both the MOR and Scorecard contain measures that are used to assess other aspects of airport performance besides screener performance, such as safety. We only consider screener performance measures to be only those that are most directly related to screener performance, which we list in the table above.

[a]TSA began deploying AITs in 2007. As of September 2012, there are approximately 700 AITs at more than 180 airports. AIT checkpoint utilization is percentage of hours during which at least one AIT machine was open.

[b]Layered security effectiveness is a composite score of two components: (1) an airport's adherence to budgeted full-time equivalent staffing levels and (2) the percentage of passengers and employees exposed to layered security techniques. Layered security includes duties in addition to passenger, carry-on and checked baggage screening that may be required, such as use of the screening of passengers by observation technique.

[c]Selectee miss rate is the percentage of selectees that are not initially screened at the checkpoint. For example, selectees include individuals on TSA's Selectee List, who are designated to receive additional screening prior to boarding an aircraft.

[d]For the Scorecard, the recertification pass rate includes only the results of the role playing scenarios conducted to assess various job functions, including physical bag searches, pat downs, and screening passengers with disabilities, and does not include the results of the assessments of a screener's threat detection skills on carry-on and checked baggage X-ray machines.

Mechanisms to Monitor Private Screener Performance Separately from Federal Screeners Could Benefit TSA

TSA does not currently monitor private screener performance separately from federal screener performance or conduct regular reviews comparing the performance of SPP and non-SPP airports. As previously noted, TSA has conducted or commissioned prior reports comparing the cost and performance of SPP and non-SPP airports. For example, in 2004 and 2007, TSA commissioned reports prepared by private consultants, while in 2008 the agency issued its own report comparing the performance of

SPP and non-SPP airports.[43] Generally, these reports found that SPP airports performed at a level equal to or better than non-SPP airports.[44] However, TSA officials stated that they do not plan to conduct similar analyses in the future, and instead, they are using across-the-board mechanisms of both private and federal screeners, such as the Scorecard, to assess screener performance across all commercial airports.

In addition to using the Scorecard, TSA conducts monthly contractor performance management reviews (PMR) at each SPP airport to assess the SPP contractor's performance against the standards set in each SPP contract.[45] The PMRs include 10 performance measures, including some of the same measures included in the Scorecard, such as TIP detection rates and recertification pass rates, for which TSA establishes acceptable quality levels of performance.[46] Failure to meet the acceptable quality levels of performance can result in corrective actions or termination of the

---

[43]In our 2009 report, we identified three limitations related to TSA's 2008 methodology for comparing screening performance at SPP and non-SPP airports. Specifically, we noted that TSA's methodology did not (1) document the rationale for including the five performance measures it reviewed; (2) control or otherwise account for other possible factors, such as airport configuration or size; and (3) provide any statistical analyses to indicate the level of confidence in the observed differences. We recommended that TSA address the limitations if it planned to use the methodology to compare performance at SPP and non-SPP airports. While TSA officials stated that they do not plan to conduct studies comparing private and federal screener performance, they stated that they would provide GAO with a description of how they would address these limitations if TSA conducts such studies in the future. As of October 2012, we have not yet received this document. See GAO-09-27R.

[44]The 2004 Bearing Point report found that the contract screening operations at the five commercial airports under the pilot program performed at the same level or better than federally screened operations. The 2007 Catapult Consultant Report found that the SPP airports in its sample performed at a level equal to or better than non-SPP airports for the four performance measures included in the analysis. The 2009 TSA study found that SPP airports in its review generally performed consistently with non-SPP in their category for the performance measures included in its analysis.

[45]The seven SPP airports in Montana are under a single contract and are, therefore, assessed together in the PMRs.

[46]The acceptable quality levels of performance vary by each airport and can be based on, for example, program policy or airport category averages for the previous year. According to agency officials, not all 10 of the performance measures in the PMRs are assessed at each of the SPP airports. For example, SPP airports that are not required to conduct layered security hours are not assessed on this performance measure.

contract.[47] For example, according to TSA officials, TSA developed reports for several of the airports that included corrective actions related to the protection of sensitive security information.

However, the Scorecard and PMR do not provide a complete picture of screener performance at SPP airports because, while both mechanisms provide a snapshot of private screener performance at each SPP airport, this information on screener performance is not summarized for the SPP as a whole or across years, which makes it difficult to identify changes in private screener performance. For example, an airport's Scorecard shows the performance of that airport during a 2-week reporting period, as well as for the year to date, in comparison with the airport's goal for each of the performance measures. However, it does not show that airport's performance in comparison with that of others in its airport category, which TSA officials explained is important when assessing screener performance. Likewise, the PMRs present information on an SPP contractor's performance against the standards in their contract during a particular month. With the exception of TIP detection rates and recertification pass rates, the PMRs do not compare an SPP airport's performance against other airports or, for example, its airport category average, which TSA officials stated is important when assessing screener performance.[48] TSA stores paper copies of the results from the performance reviews, but it does not transfer the information into an electronic system or format that would allow the agency to easily review SPP performance over time. During the course of our audit work, TSA officials informed us that they have identified this as an area needing improvement and plan to introduce a new tool to collect and consolidate this information in fiscal year 2013, but were unable to provide specific

---

[47]For SPP contractors whose contract allows for an award fee, TSA conducts a semi-annual evaluation to determine the amount of the award fee earned during that 6-month period. The formula for the award fee is based on a subset of the measures used in the PMRs. According to TSA officials, contracts that allow for award fees enable TSA to reward contractors for exceeding the conditions set forth in their contract and are available only at the larger SPP airports. As of August 2012, San Francisco International Airport (category X) and Kansas City International Airport (category I) are the only SPP airports whose contracts allow for award fees.

[48]While it is useful for TSA managers to compare an SPP airport's performance against its airport category for TIP detection rate and recertification pass rate in the PMRs, it is also important that the set of measures used to compare screener performance at SPP and non-SPP airports address a variety of agency priorities, such as passenger satisfaction. For more on the key attributes of successful performance measures, see appendix V.

information on the format of this tool and how it will be used. Further, neither the Scorecard nor the PMR provides information on performance in prior years nor controls for variables that TSA officials explained to us are important when comparing private and federal screener performance, such as the type of X-ray machine used for TIP detection rates.

Monitoring private screener performance in comparison with federal screener performance is consistent with the statutory requirement that TSA enter into a contract with a private screening company only if the Administrator determines and certifies to Congress that the level of screening services and protection provided at an airport under a contract will be equal to or greater than the level that would be provided at the airport by federal government personnel.[49] Further, according to TSA guidance on the SPP, one of TSA's major goals for the SPP is that private screeners must perform at the same or better level as federal screeners. A mechanism to monitor private versus federal screener performance would better position TSA to know whether the level of screening services and protection provided at SPP airports continues to be equal to or greater than the level provided at non-SPP airports. TSA officials stated that it is not TSA's goal to ensure that SPP airports continue to perform at levels equal to or greater than non-SPP airports, but to ensure that all airports operate at their optimal level, which they monitor using across-the-board mechanisms, such as the Scorecard. However, monitoring private versus federal screener performance could also help TSA to identify positive or negative trends in SPP performance that could lead to improvements in the program and TSA's monitoring of SPP airports in general, and inform decision-making regarding potential future expansion of the SPP.

Conclusions

TSA faces a daunting task in ensuring that a screening workforce is in place to consistently implement security protocols across the nation's commercial airports while facilitating passenger travel. Questions about the performance of private screeners compared with federal screeners, recently enacted statutory provisions, and changes to the program's application and approval process underscore the need for TSA to ensure that the program's application requirements are clearly defined and

---

[49]See 49 U.S.C. § 44920(d) (providing further that private screening companies must be owned and controlled by a citizen of the United States, subject to a waiver of this requirement by the TSA Administrator in certain circumstances).

consistently applied so that aviation stakeholders have a full and fair opportunity to participate in the program. Thus, a well-defined and clearly documented application guideline that states (1) the criteria and process that TSA is using to assess airport's participation in the SPP, (2) how TSA will obtain and analyze cost information regarding screening cost-efficiency and effectiveness and the implications of not responding to related application questions, and (3) specific examples of additional information airports should consider providing to TSA to help assess airports' suitability for SPP could benefit TSA. Specifically, guidelines could help alleviate airports' uncertainty about the application process and better inform TSA to determine whether to approve an airport's SPP application.

It is also incumbent on TSA to be capable of determining if airports participating in the program are performing at a level that is equal to or greater than the level of security that would be provided by federal screeners at the airports through regular monitoring and reporting. Although not a prerequisite for approving an application for participation in the SPP, TSA must certify to Congress that the level of screening services and protection provided by a private screening contractor will be equal to or greater than the level that would be provided at the airport by federal government personnel before entering into a contract with a private screening company. While TSA regularly tracks screener performance at all airports and reevaluates the measures it uses to assess this performance, TSA has not conducted regular reviews comparing private and federal screener performance and does not have plans to do so. Regular comparison reviews would enable TSA to know whether the level of screening services provided by private screening contractors is equal to or greater than the level provided at non-SPP airports. These reviews could also assist TSA in identifying performance changes that could lead to improvements in the program and inform decision making regarding potential expansion of the SPP.

Recommendations for Executive Action

To improve TSA's SPP application process and to inform decisions regarding the future of the SPP, we recommend that the Secretary of the Department of Homeland Security direct the Administrator of TSA to take the following two actions:

- develop guidance that clearly (1) states the criteria and process that TSA is using to assess whether participation in the SPP would compromise security or detrimentally affect the cost-efficiency or the effectiveness of the screening of passengers or property at the airport; (2) states how TSA will obtain and analyze cost information regarding screening cost-efficiency and effectiveness and the implications of not responding to the related application questions; and (3) provides specific examples of additional information airports should consider providing to TSA to help assess an airport's suitability for SPP, and

- develop a mechanism to regularly monitor private versus federal screener performance.

Agency Comments and Our Evaluation

We requested comments on a draft of the sensitive version of this report from TSA. On November 7, 2012, DHS provided written comments, which are reprinted in appendix VI and provided technical comments, which we incorporated as appropriate. DHS generally concurred with our two recommendations and described actions planned to address them. Specifically,

- DHS stated that TSA will provide as much information as is prudent on how the agency would evaluate if an airport's participation in the SPP would compromise security or detrimentally affect the cost-efficiency or the effectiveness of the screening of passengers or property at the airport. Further, DHS stated that TSA will provide general categories of information in the SPP application guidance it plans to issue and will continually review the guidance to ensure that airports are comfortable with the SPP application process and understand how all the information provided will be used to evaluate their application. TSA expects to post an overview of the SPP application process to the agency's website by November 30, 2012, that would specify details on the data it will use to assess applications and discuss its cost-estimating methodology and definition of cost efficiency. We believe that these are beneficial steps that would address our recommendation once adopted, and help address stakeholder concerns about the transparency of the SPP application process.

- DHS stated that starting in the first quarter of fiscal year 2013, TSA will produce semi-annual reports that will include an evaluation of SPP airport performance against the performance of TSA airports as a whole, as well as performance against each SPP airport category. Additionally, DHS noted that TSA is in the initial planning phase of deploying an electronic data collection system to facilitate systematic collection and reporting of SPP data, as well as TSA oversight of SPP contractor activities.

Deployment of the electronic data collection system is targeted for the latter part of fiscal year 2013. Once implemented, these new reporting mechanisms will address our recommendation by facilitating TSA's efforts to assess private versus federal screener performance.

We are sending copies of this report to the Secretary of Homeland Security, the TSA Administrator, the House Infrastructure and Transportation Committee, and other interested parties. In addition, the report is available at no charge on the GAO web-site at http://www.gao.gov.

If you or your staff have any questions concerning this report, please contact me at (202) 512-4379 or at lords@gao.gov. Contact points for our Offices of Congressional Relations and Public Affairs may be found on that last page of this report. GAO staff who made major contributions to this report are listed in appendix VII.

Sincerely Yours,

Stephen M. Lord
Director, Homeland Security and Justice Issues

Appendix I: Objectives, Scope, and Methodology

<table>
<tr><td>

Objectives

</td><td>

This appendix describes how we did our work to address (1) the status of Screening Partnership Program (SPP) applications, and airport operator, other stakeholder, and the Transportation Security Administration's (TSA) views on the advantages and disadvantages of participating in the SPP; (2) the extent to which TSA has provided guidance to govern the SPP application process; and (3) the extent to which TSA assesses and monitors the performance of private and federal screeners.

</td></tr>
<tr><td>

Scope and Methodology

</td><td>

To address all three of these objectives, we interviewed Federal Security Directors (FSD); airport operators; screeners; and where applicable, SPP contractors at 10 airports. We selected the 10 airports by matching an SPP to a non-SPP airport, in each of the five airport categories (category X, I, II, III, and IV), based primarily on (1) annual passenger and baggage volumes, (2) screener staffing model full-time equivalent allocation, and (3) number of check-points and screening lanes.[1] Additionally, on the basis of available travel resources, we visited 7 of the 10 airports to observe airport screening operations, including any unique challenges faced by these airports. We surveyed the 28 airport operators who have applied to the SPP since its inception up until April 2012 to obtain their perspectives on the SPP application process, the advantages and disadvantages of participating in private or federal screening, and performance measures TSA uses to assess screeners. The 28 airports whose airport operators we surveyed include 16 from airports that were participating in the SPP at the time of the survey, 2 airports that withdrew their applications before TSA made a decision, 3 airports that were approved but never transitioned to the SPP because commercial airline service was discontinued at the airport, and 7 airports that initially applied from March 2009 through April 2012 (when we implemented our survey).[2] A 29th airport, Bozeman Yellowstone International Airport, applied to the SPP for the first time in June 2012 and therefore was not included in our survey. Two airport operators did not respond to our survey. One of the 2

</td></tr>
</table>

---

[1] TSA classifies commercial airports in the United States into one of five security risk categories (X, I, II, III, and IV) based on various factors, such as the total number of takeoffs and landings annually, and other special security considerations. In general, category X airports have the largest number of passenger boardings, and category IV airports have the smallest.

[2] Of the 7 airports that applied to the SPP for the first time from March 2009 through April 2012, 6 were evaluated under TSA's "clear and substantial advantage" standard and the seventh was evaluated in accordance with the provisions of the FAA Modernization Act.

was an airport that had withdrawn its application to the SPP before a
decision was made and a second an airport whose application was
denied in January 2011 while the "clear and substantial advantage"
application standard was in effect. We conducted two expert reviews of
the survey with major aviation associations, and three survey pretests
with airport operators. In addition to the 28 airport operators in our survey,
we also interviewed the airport operators of Bozeman Yellowstone
International Airport and the 5 non-SPP airports we visited to obtain their
perspectives on the potential advantages and disadvantages of
participating in the SPP. For this study, our focus is on assessing airport
screening performance as opposed to individual screener performance.
We assessed the aggregate of individual screener performance
measures only to the extent that they reflect overall screening
performance at airports.

To determine the status of SPP applications, and airport operator, other
stakeholders', and TSA's views on the advantages and disadvantages of
participating in the SPP, we interviewed officials of TSA's SPP Program
Management Office (PMO) and reviewed the 15 SPP applications that
had been submitted since fiscal year 2009, as well as TSA's available
decision memos on the applications.[3] We also analyzed the results of our
survey of SPP airport operators and operators of airports that have
applied to the SPP. We also conducted semistructured interviews with
TSA, contractor, and airport officials during our airport site visit interviews
as well as interviewed aviation industry stakeholders to identify the
advantages and disadvantages of using federal and nonfederal
screeners.

To determine the extent to which TSA has provided guidance to govern
the SPP application process, we reviewed key statutes and policies to
identify requirements related to the SPP. We also analyzed past and
current SPP application forms and instructions, as well as interviewed
TSA headquarters officials, to identify the requirements and process for
applying to the SPP. As previously noted, we surveyed airport operators,
which included operators of all 16 SPP airports and the 6 airports whose
applications TSA denied for not establishing that transitioning to the SPP
would provide a "clear and substantial advantage to TSA security

---

[3]Decision memos were not available for all SPP applicants because, for example, they
were not prepared or were lost when TSA transferred to a new file share program.

operations," to determine their perspectives on the SPP application
process. Further, we interviewed airport officials at the 8 airports that
have applied to the SPP since 2009, which includes the 6 airports that
applied under TSA's "clear and substantial advantage" standard, to obtain
their perspectives on the clarity of the SPP application process. We also
compared TSA's application process and requirements against standards
in *Standards for Internal Control in the Federal Government* which calls
for an agency's transactions and other significant events to be clearly
documented and well defined.[4]

To determine the extent to which TSA assesses and monitors the
performance of private and federal screeners, we reviewed TSA's
screener performance measurement documents, reports, and data
systems. We also interviewed TSA headquarters officials knowledgeable
about TSA's performance management process to identify current
screener performance measures. At the airports we visited, we observed
screening operations to identify areas where screener performance could
be assessed, and interviewed contractor, airport, and TSA officials to
obtain their perspectives on the current set of performance measures. We
reviewed TSA's most recent set of performance measures in the Office of
Security Operations Executive Scorecard as well as its previous set in the
Management Objective Report to determine what, if any, improvements
had been made. To do so, we evaluated the sets of measures against the
nine key attributes of successful performance measures, which we
developed in prior reports based on GAO's prior efforts to examine
agencies that were successful in implementing the performance
measurement aspects of the Government Performance and Results Act
(GPRA).[5] We also evaluated TSA's process for assessing and monitoring
the performance of federal and private screeners against standards in
Standards for Internal Control in the Federal Government and best
practices for performance management.[6]

To determine how screener performance compares at SPP and non-SPP
airports, we compared screener performance for all 16 SPP airports with
the average performance of airports in their category, as well as

---

[4]GAO/AIMD-00-21.3.1.

[5]GAO-03-143.

[6]GAO/AIMD-00-21.3.1, GAO/GGD-96-118, and GAO-03-143.

nationally, from fiscal year 2009 through 2011. For our comparison, we focused on four performance measures: threat image projection (TIP) detection rates;[7] recertification pass rates;[8] aviation screening assessment program (ASAP) covert test results;[9] and presence, advisement, communication, and execution (PACE) evaluation results.[10] We selected these measures primarily based on our review of previous studies that compared screener performance of SPP and non-SPP airports as well as on our interviews with aviation security subject matter experts, including TSA's FSD, SPP contractors, and airport and aviation industry stakeholders. We also selected performance measures for which TSA has, for the most part, consistently and systematically collected data for our study years. For some of the measures we selected, such as PACE evaluations, data were not available for all 3 years or all airports; nonetheless, we selected these measures because they represent integral aspects of screener performance. We explain these circumstances further when we present the data. To ensure the reliability of the performance measures data, we (1) interviewed TSA officials who use and maintain the data; (2) checked the data for missing information, outliers, and obvious errors; and (3) reviewed documentation for the relevant data systems to ensure the data's integrity. On the basis of the steps we took, we found the data reliable for the purpose of providing summary statistics of screener performance for the four performance measures we analyzed. However, as noted earlier in this report, there are

---

[7]The TIP system is designed to test private and federal screeners' detection capabilities by projecting threat images, including images of guns and explosives, into bags as they are screened. Private and federal screeners are responsible for positively identifying the threat image and calling for the bag to be searched.

[8]Private and federal screeners must pass annual standardized recertification tests composed of image, job knowledge, and standard operating procedures tests.

[9]ASAP tests are covert tests conducted by TSA at both screening checkpoints and checked baggage screening areas. ASAP tests are implemented locally by unrecognizable role players who attempt to pass threat objects, such as knives, guns, or simulated improvised explosive devices, through the screening checkpoints or onto the plane in their checked baggage. The tests are designed to assess the operational effectiveness of screeners.

[10]PACE evaluations assess the level of standardization across airports in the following four areas: presence (i.e., command presence), advisement (i.e., telling passengers what to do), communication, and execution. PACE evaluators visit a checkpoint covertly and assess the screening personnel on a variety of elements, such as whether the officers provide comprehensive instruction and engage passengers in a calm and respectful manner when screening.

many factors, some of which cannot be controlled for, that may account for differences in screener performance; therefore, the differences we found in screener performance at SPP and non-SPP airports may not be attributed entirely to the use of either federal or private screeners.

Appendix II: TSA's Screening Partnership Program Application History

As of October 2012, 29 airports have applied for participation in the SPP since the inception of the program in 2004 (see table 3).

Table 3: SPP Application History

Airport	Airport Code	Category	Application history
Elko Municipal, NV	EKO	IV	Applied 11/04, withdrew 10/05
Jackson Hole, WY	JAC	II	Applied 1/05, approved 5/05
Kansas City International, MO	MCI	I	Applied 4/05, approved 5/05
Greater Rochester International, NY	ROC	I	Applied 4/05, approved 5/05
San Francisco International, CA	SFO	X	Applied 4/05, approved 5/05
Tupelo Regional, MS	TUP	IV	Applied 4/05, approved 5/05
Joe Foss Field, SD	FSD	II	Applied 4/05, approved 12/07
Key West International, FL	EYW	II	Applied 10/06, approved 5/07
Florida Keys Marathon, FL	MTH	IV	Applied 10/06, approved 5/07
Charles M. Schulz-Sonoma County, CA	STS	III	Applied 11/06, approved 6/07
E. 34th Street Heliport, NY	6N5	IV	Applied 1/07, approved 1/07
Gallup Municipal, NM	GUP	IV	Applied 5/07, approved 10/07
Roswell International, NM	ROW	IV	Applied 6/07, approved 10/07
L.M. Clayton/Wolf Point, MT	OLF	IV	Applied 12/07, approved 8/09
Sidney-Richland Municipal, MT	SDY	IV	Applied 12/07, approved 8/09
Glasgow International/Wokal Field, MT	GGW	IV	Applied 1/08, approved 8/09
Dawson Community, MT	GDV	IV	Applied 1/08, approved 8/09
Frank Wiley Field, MT	MLS	IV	Applied 1/08, approved 8/09
Lewistown Municipal, MT	LWT	IV	Applied 1/08, approved 8/09
Havre City-County, MT	HVR	IV	Applied 1/08, approved 8/09
Branson, MO	BBG	III	Applied 10/08, withdrew 3/09
Bert Mooney, MT	BTM	III	Applied 3/09, denied 1/11, applied 7/11, denied 1/12, applied 6/12, approved 8/12
West Yellowstone, MT	WYS	IV	Applied 9/09, denied 1/11, applied 7/11, approved 1/12
Glacier Park International, MT	GPI	III	Applied 10/09, denied 1/11, applied 3/12, approved 6/12
Missoula International, MT	MSO	II	Applied 5/10, denied 1/11
Springfield/Branson National, MO	SGF	II	Applied 12/10, denied 1/11
Orlando Sanford International, FL	SFB	II	Applied 2/11, denied 6/11, applied 12/11, denied 2/12, applied 2/12, approved 6/12
Sacramento International, CA	SMF	I	Applied 2/12[a], approved 7/12
Bozeman Yellowstone International, MT	BZN	II	Applied 6/12, approved 8/12

Source: GAO analysis of TSA information

Notes: The SPP was launched in 2004. The "clear and substantial advantage" standard was announced in January 2011 and was used to evaluate applications submitted from March 2009 through February 2011. The FAA Modernization and Reform Act of 2012, Pub. L. No. 112-95, § 803, 126 Stat. 11, 135-36, was enacted in February 2012. San Francisco International Airport, Kansas City International Airport, Greater Rochester International Airport, Jackson Hole Airport, and Tupelo Regional Airport participated in TSA's 2-year pilot program using private screening companies to screen passengers and checked baggage. See 49 U.S.C. § 44919. Upon completion of the pilot program, TSA established a permanent program named the Screening Partnership Program to which all five of these airports then applied. See 49 U.S.C. § 44920.

[a]Sacramento International Airport submitted its first application to the SPP approximately 1 week before the FAA Modernization Act was enacted. In March 2012, TSA revised the SPP application to facilitate compliance with provisions of the act and requested that Sacramento International Airport resubmit its application using the new application form. While the airport submitted its new application form in April 2012, TSA considers the date of receipt to still be February 2012.

As of October 2012, 16 airports are participating in the SPP and 6 airports were recently approved for participation (see figure 4 and table 4).

Figure 4: Airports Participating in or Recently Approved for Participation in the Screening Partnership Program (SPP)

Airport category

★ Category X

◎ Category I

◆ Category II

▢ Category III

✪ Category IV

Source: GAO analysis of TSA information

Note: TSA classifies commercial airports in the United States into one of five security risk categories (X, I, II, III, and IV) based on various factors, such as the total number of takeoffs and landings annually, and other special security considerations. In general, category X airports have the largest number of passenger boardings, and category IV airports have the smallest.

Table 4: Airports Participating in or Recently Approved for Participation in the Screening Partnership Program (SPP)

Airport	Airport Code	Category	Status
Jackson Hole, WY	JAC	II	Currently participating
Kansas City International, MO	MCI	I	Currently participating
Greater Rochester International, NY	ROC	I	Currently participating
San Francisco International, CA	SFO	X	Currently participating
Tupelo Regional, MS	TUP	IV	Currently participating
Joe Foss Field, SD	FSD	II	Currently participating
Key West International, FL	EYW	II	Currently participating
Charles M. Schulz-Sonoma County, CA	STS	III	Currently participating
Roswell International, NM	ROW	IV	Currently participating
L.M. Clayton/Wolf Point, MT	OLF	IV	Currently participating
Sidney-Richland Municipal, MT	SDY	IV	Currently participating
Glasgow International/Wokal Field, MT	GGW	IV	Currently participating
Dawson Community, MT	GDV	IV	Currently participating
Frank Wiley Field, MT	MLS	IV	Currently participating
Lewistown Municipal, MT	LWT	IV	Currently participating
Havre City-County, MT	HVR	IV	Currently participating
Bert Mooney, MT	BTM	III	Approved pending contract
West Yellowstone, MT	WYS	IV	Approved pending contract
Glacier Park International, MT	GPI	III	Approved pending contract
Orlando Sanford International, FL	SFB	II	Approved pending contract
Sacramento International, CA	SMF	I	Approved pending contract
Bozeman Yellowstone International, MT	BZN	II	Approved pending contract

Source: GAO Analysis of TSA information.

Appendix IV: Other Measures to Assess Screener Performance

TSA collects data on several other performance measures, but, for various reasons, they cannot be used to compare private and federal screener performance for the purposes of our review. Below, we discuss four variables occasionally cited by the airport officials and aviation stakeholders we interviewed as possible measures for comparing federal and private screening and the reasons we did not use them to compare private and federal screener performance.

- **Wait times:** A wait time is the total cycle time for a passenger to reach the advanced imaging technology (AIT) machine or walkthrough metal detector (whichever is available) from entering the queue. TSA officials at some airports collect these data by passing out a card to a passenger at the end of the line. We do not present passenger wait time data because we found that TSA's policy for collecting wait times changed during the time period of our analyses and that these data were not collected in a consistent manner across all airports.[1] Further, TSA officials noted that wait times are affected by a number of variables that TSA cannot control, such as airline flight schedules.

- **Passenger throughput:** Passenger throughput is the number of passengers screened in each of the screening lanes per hour. These data are collected automatically by the screening machines. TSA officials stated that they review this measure to ensure that passengers are not being screened too quickly, which may mean that screeners are not being thorough, or are screened too slowly, which may mean that screeners could be more efficient. According to TSA officials, passenger throughput is affected by a number of factors that are unique to individual airports, including technology, capacity and configuration of the checkpoint, type of traveler, and various factors related to the flight schedules. While officials noted that there is a goal for how many passengers should be screened per hour, a rate below this goal is not necessarily indicative of a problem, but could be due to a reduced passenger volume, as is likely during nonpeak travel hours. For example, at one of the airports we visited, there are few flights

---

[1]TSA's policy for measuring wait time changed in March 2010. Instead of collecting precise wait times every hour, TSA began only recording instances in which the wait time was more than 20 or 30 minutes. Further, through our site visits, we learned that airports collect wait time data in different ways. For example, some airports calculate the wait time from the end of the queue until the passenger reaches the travel document checker podium; other airports calculate the time from the end of the line until the passenger passes through the walkthrough metal detector after being screened or the AIT.

scheduled for the morning and evening, at which point passenger throughput is very low, and several flights scheduled around lunchtime, at which point the passenger throughput is relatively high.

- **Human capital measures:** We also considered reviewing human capital measures such as attrition, absenteeism, and injury rates. However, TSA's Office of Human Capital does not collect these data for SPP airports because, according to these officials, maintaining information on human capital measures is the sole responsibility of the contractor. While the contractors collect and report this information to TSA, TSA does not validate the accuracy of the self-reported data. Further, TSA does not require that the contractors use the same human capital measures as TSA, and accordingly, differences may exist in how the metrics are defined and how the data are collected. Therefore, TSA cannot guarantee that a comparison of SPP and non-SPP airports on these human capital metrics would be an equal comparison. TSA officials also stated that they do not use human capital measures to compare SPP and non-SPP airports because these measures are affected by variables that are not within the control of TSA or the contractor. For example, some airports are located in areas that have a high cost of living, and as a result, it can be difficult to hire screeners because the screener salary may not be competitive there.

- **"Red team" covert tests:** In addition to ASAP tests, TSA's Office of Inspections also conducts covert tests, the results of which are also classified. These covert tests are commonly referred to as red team tests, and are designed to identify potential vulnerabilities in TSA's screening operations, as opposed to test screeners' compliance with standard operating procedures. We have previously reported that an airport's red team test results represent a snapshot in time and should not be considered a comprehensive measurement of any one airport's performance or any individual airport's performance. Further, while GAO analyzed red team tests in these reports, we determined, for reasons we cannot report here due to the sensitive security nature of the information, that it would not be appropriate to analyze the tests for the purpose of comparing screener performance at SPP and non-SPP airports.

Appendix V: GAO's Assessment of Screener Performance Measures

By adding measures to the Scorecard that addressed other non-security-related TSA priorities, TSA improved the set of performance measures it uses to asses screener performance. In the past, we have examined agencies that were successful in implementing the performance measurement aspects of the Government Performance and Results Act and concluded that these agencies exhibit certain key characteristics that it characterized as the nine key attributes of successful performance measures.[1] While the Management Objective Report (MOR) addressed eight of the key attributes, it did not address balance because the set of performance measures did not address a variety of agency priorities. Balance among a set of performance measures is important because it helps to ensure that performance measurement efforts are not overemphasizing one or two priorities at the expense of others, which may keep managers from understanding the effectiveness of their program in supporting the agency's overall missions and goals. Specifically, the MOR did not contain measures related to passenger satisfaction which, according to TSA's Strategic Plan, is part of the agency's mission.[2] However, the Office of Security Operations (OSO) Executive Scorecard (Scorecard) includes passenger satisfaction measures, such as the number of negative and positive customer contacts made to the TSA Contact Center through e-mails or phone calls per 100,000 passengers screened through the airport, which were not previously included in the MOR.[3] By adding measures related to passenger satisfaction to the Scorecard, TSA ensured balance in the set of performance measures the agency uses to assess screener performance and thereby ensured that its assessment of screening operation performance would be representative of a variety of program and agency goals (see table 5).

---

[1] According to the GPRA, as amended, federal agencies should set program goals, measure performance against those goals, and report publicly on their progress. See 31 U.S.C. § 1115. While GPRA focuses on the agency level, performance goals and measures are important management tools for all levels of an agency, such as the program or activity level, and accordingly, GAO's key attributes are applicable at those levels as well. For more on the key attributes, see GAO-04-143.

[2] According to TSA's fiscal year 2005-2009 Strategic Plan, the agency's most recent strategic plan as of July 2012, TSA strives to balance security with customer service.

[3] The TSA Contact Center handles these customer contacts for all of TSA, not only those related to passenger and baggage screening. The passenger satisfaction metrics in the Scorecard do not include other types of customer contacts made by passengers, such as via comment cards at local airports or letters written to the TSA Administrator.

Table 5: GAO's Analysis of the Management Objective Report and Executive Scorecard against the Key Attributes of Successful Performance Measures

Attribute	Definition	GAO's assessment	
		MOR	Scorecard
Linkage	Performance goals and measures should align with an agency's or program's goals and mission.	√	√
Clarity	Performance measures have clarity when they are clearly stated and do not contain extraneous elements.	√	√
Measurable Target	Where appropriate, performance measures should have quantifiable targets to facilitate comparisons between projected performance and actual results and be reasonable predictors of desired outcomes.	√	√
Objectivity	Measures should be reasonably free of significant bias that would distort the accurate assessment of performance.	√	√
Reliability	Measures should be amenable to applying standard procedures for collecting data or calculating results so that they would likely produce the same results if repeated.	√	√
Core Program Activities	Performance measures should be scoped to evaluate the activities that an entity is expected to perform to support the program.	√	√
Limited Overlap	Measures overlap when the results of multiple measures provide basically the same information, which does provide any benefit to program management.	√	√
Balance	Balance exists when a suite of measures ensures that an organization's various priorities are addressed.	X Does not address customer service	√
Government- wide Priorities	Performance measures should cover a range of related performance measures to address government wide priorities, such as quality, timeliness, and efficiency.	This attribute is not applicable because TSA and DHS may address government-wide priorities through its other missions.	

Key: √ = Addressed, X= Not addressed

Source: GAO Analysis of TSA documents

Note: Both the MOR and the Scorecard contain measures that are used to assess other aspects of airport performance besides screener performance, such as safety. For this analysis, we selected the measures most directly related to screener performance.

Appendix VI: Comments from the Department of Homeland Security

U.S. Department of Homeland Security
Washington, DC 20528

Homeland
Security

November 7, 2012

Stephen M. Lord
Director, Homeland Security and Justice Issues
U.S. Government Accountability Office
441 G Street, NW
Washington, DC 20548

Re: GAO Draft Report 13-16, "SCREENING PARTNERSHIP PROGRAM: TSA Should
        Issue More Guidance to Airports and Monitor Private versus Federal Screener
        Performance"

Dear Mr. Lord:

Thank you for the opportunity to review and comment on this draft report. The U.S. Department of Homeland Security (DHS) appreciates the U.S. Government Accountability Office's (GAO's) work in planning and conducting its review and issuing this report.

Private contract screeners have made important contributions to the Transportation Security Administration's (TSA's) mission of protecting the Nation's transportation systems since TSA's inception in 2001. These contributions continue today as these screeners actively screen more than 28 million passengers and their baggage annually. Applying for participation in the Screening Partnership Program (SPP) is voluntary, which presents a difficulty in ensuring airport operators have the information they need and want. For that reason, the GAO survey of these operators provides valuable insight for shaping the information and guidance TSA provides about the program.

Given the nature of the statutes governing the SPP, definitively determining differences in performance between private contract and federal screeners is also difficult. TSA found discussions with GAO concerning performance measurement and data collection productive and beneficial. We appreciate the tremendous effort GAO put forth in reviewing several years' worth of reliable performance data, validating the appropriateness of the measures TSA uses, and confirming TSA's conclusions concerning the performance of SPP and non-SPP airports. GAO found that while some SPP airports perform slightly better than the category average, others perform slightly below others in their respective categories. Most importantly, the report notes that differences in performance cannot be entirely attributed to use of federal or private screeners. TSA does not expect to definitively determine if private contract screeners perform better or worse than federal counterparts with respect to approving or denying applications. Future applications will continue to be evaluated in accordance with applicable statutes.

We also appreciate GAO's acknowledgment of the improvements TSA has made in its set of screener performance measures during 2012 by including measures that address passenger satisfaction. As noted in the report, these measures address all aspects of TSA's airport screening strategic goals and mission. In addition, as noted in the report, TSA has monitored and evaluated airport performance since creating the Performance Measurement Information System in 2001. Since then, performance management within TSA has matured at all levels, and the Office of Security Operation's Performance Management Branch (PMB) is specifically dedicated to monitoring, evaluating, and reporting performance at all TSA airports, including SPP airports. The PMB has collaborated with the SPP office and has repeatedly evaluated the performance of federal and private screener performance as comparable and compliant with provisions of 49 U.S.C § 44920 that "the level of screening services and protection provided ... will be equal to or greater than the level that would be provided at the airport by Federal Government personnel."

As noted in the report, the *Federal Aviation Administration (FAA) Modernization and Reform Act of 2012* provided several standards that TSA must use when determining whether to approve an application, a timeline for approving or denying an application, and specific actions to take if an application is denied. TSA quickly revised the program application, as well as its application process, to comply with the statute. Five airports applied to join the program within weeks of the President signing the Act. TSA's response to the near concurrent passage of the Act and application submission was vigorous, and TSA met the timeline of approving or denying an application within 120 days for all airports. In fact, decisions to approve all five applications were made in less than 85 days.

Since the introduction of SPP, TSA has provided guidance to airport operators on the nature of the program, the application process, general program news, and answers to frequently asked questions. This information has been available via TSA's Web site, www.TSA.gov, and is frequently updated to ensure the information's accuracy and relevancy. In addition, program officials are available to discuss the program and the application process with airport operators. Further, program officials have discussed the program at length on numerous occasions with airports and airport boards, and the report notes that airport operators have expressed that the Program Management Office was helpful in providing general information. Finally, each airport's Federal Security Director can and does discuss the program and application process with respective airport personnel.

In recent months, the SPP office has undergone a transformation precipitated by the *FAA Modernization and Reform Act of 2012*, and strides have been made to improve many aspects of the program. GAO's review and recommendations are key pieces of this transformation.

The draft report contained two recommendations with which DHS concurs. Specifically, GAO recommended that the Secretary of Homeland Security direct the Administrator of TSA to:

Recommendation 1: Develop guidance that clearly (i) states the criteria and process that TSA is using to assess whether participation in the SPP would compromise security or detrimentally affect the cost efficiency or the effectiveness of the screening of passengers or property at the airport; (ii) states how TSA will obtain and analyze cost information regarding screening cost efficiency and effectiveness and the implications of not responding to the related application

2

questions; and (iii) provides specific examples of additional information airports should consider providing to TSA to help assess an airport's suitability for SPP.

Response: Concur. TSA believes that completely addressing all aspects of the recommendation may not be feasible. Parts (i) and (iii) of the recommendation may prove difficult to faithfully address, though TSA will rigorously address the spirit of both parts.

With respect to part (i) of the recommendation to develop guidance on the application process, the standard that approving the application would not "compromise security" or "detrimentally affect ... the effectiveness" of screening is extremely broad and difficult to define. Given the changing nature of threats to aviation, security may be compromised on the basis of several pieces of information that independently are innocuous, but taken in concert are critical. However, TSA will provide as much information as is prudent on how that standard will be evaluated.

With respect to part (iii) of the recommendation to develop guidance on the application process, providing specific examples of information to be considered by airports may prove problematic. TSA has no preconceived notion of what information an airport may want to provide. TSA will provide general categories of information and continuously review its guidance on this subject to ensure airports feel comfortable with the process and understand how all the information they provide will be used.

By November 30, 2012, TSA expects to post an overview of the application process that addresses the recommendation to the TSA Web site. Specifically, the overview will describe the process, provide as many details as possible concerning the data that will be used to approve or deny an application, and discuss TSA's cost-estimating methodology and TSA's definition of cost efficiency.

TSA is currently revising its application as to comply with appropriate federal records management directives. This effort should be completed early in calendar year 2013. TSA will post the new application to the Web site immediately following Office of Management and Budget approval. In the interim, the current application (revised in March of 2012) will remain available to the public. As part of this effort, TSA will also review the GAO survey of airport operators in order to tailor the application instructions and overview of the process to ensure potential applicants understand the process.

Following enactment of the *FAA Modernization and Reform Act of 2012*, TSA began revising its application process to ensure compliance. This effort ran concurrently with receiving and making determinations for five applications—all applications were approved within the 120-day timeline. Completion of the revised application process, including processes to follow if an application is denied, is expected during the fall of 2012. Once final, TSA will provide the application process documentation to GAO.

3

Recommendation 2: Develop a mechanism to regularly monitor private versus federal screener performance.

Response: Concur. Beginning in the first quarter of Fiscal Year (FY) 2013, TSA will produce reports semi-annually, evaluating compliance with all provisions of the statute. This report will include an evaluation of SPP airport performance against the performance of TSA as a whole, as well as performance against its airport category. To evaluate performance criteria that are reasonably within the control of the contractor, TSA will use measures that are meaningful, provide value to TSA, are uniformly applied all airports, and, to the extent practicable, are not influenced by factors outside a contractor's control such as airport layout.

Finally, the SPP is investigating the deployment of an electronic data collection system to facilitate systematic collection and reporting of data from across the program. The project is in the initial planning phases, with a potential deployment targeted for the latter part of FY 2013. Goals of the system are to allow contractors to submit some deliverables online, allow data collection and reporting from monthly performance reviews, and facilitate TSA oversight of contractor activities in a systematic and uniform way. Data reliability will be a key component, and the system will incorporate best practices to ensure the accuracy and reliability of the data. The program expects the system to integrate with other the TSA enterprise-wide tools, such as the Performance Information Management System, a business intelligence tool, to facilitate rapid data analysis and performance evaluation using disparate data sources.

Again, thank you for the opportunity to review and comment on this draft report. Technical comments were previously provided under separate cover. Please feel free to contact me if you have any questions. We look forward to working with you in the future.

Sincerely,

Jim H. Crumpacker
Director
Departmental GAO-OIG Liaison Office

4

Appendix VII: GAO Contact and Staff Acknowledgments

GAO Contact	Stephen M. Lord, (202) 512-4379 or lords@gao.gov
Acknowledgments	In addition to the contact named above, Glenn Davis, Assistant Director, and Edith Sohna, Analyst-in-Charge, managed this assignment. Erin O'Brien and Michelle Woods made significant contributions to the work. Carl Barden, Stuart Kaufman, Stanley Kostyla, and Minette Richardson assisted with design and methodology. Tom Lombardi provided legal support. Linda Miller provided assistance in report preparation, and Lydia Araya made contributions to the graphics presented in the report.

GAO's Mission	The Government Accountability Office, the audit, evaluation, and investigative arm of Congress, exists to support Congress in meeting its constitutional responsibilities and to help improve the performance and accountability of the federal government for the American people. GAO examines the use of public funds; evaluates federal programs and policies; and provides analyses, recommendations, and other assistance to help Congress make informed oversight, policy, and funding decisions. GAO's commitment to good government is reflected in its core values of accountability, integrity, and reliability.
Obtaining Copies of GAO Reports and Testimony	The fastest and easiest way to obtain copies of GAO documents at no cost is through GAO's website (http://www.gao.gov). Each weekday afternoon, GAO posts on its website newly released reports, testimony, and correspondence. To have GAO e-mail you a list of newly posted products, go to http://www.gao.gov and select "E-mail Updates."
Order by Phone	The price of each GAO publication reflects GAO's actual cost of production and distribution and depends on the number of pages in the publication and whether the publication is printed in color or black and white. Pricing and ordering information is posted on GAO's website, http://www.gao.gov/ordering.htm. Place orders by calling (202) 512-6000, toll free (866) 801-7077, or TDD (202) 512-2537. Orders may be paid for using American Express, Discover Card, MasterCard, Visa, check, or money order. Call for additional information.
Connect with GAO	Connect with GAO on Facebook, Flickr, Twitter, and YouTube. Subscribe to our RSS Feeds or E-mail Updates. Listen to our Podcasts. Visit GAO on the web at www.gao.gov.
To Report Fraud, Waste, and Abuse in Federal Programs	Contact: Website: http://www.gao.gov/fraudnet/fraudnet.htm E-mail: fraudnet@gao.gov Automated answering system: (800) 424-5454 or (202) 512-7470
Congressional Relations	Katherine Siggerud, Managing Director, siggerudk@gao.gov, (202) 512-4400, U.S. Government Accountability Office, 441 G Street NW, Room 7125, Washington, DC 20548
Public Affairs	Chuck Young, Managing Director, youngc1@gao.gov, (202) 512-4800 U.S. Government Accountability Office, 441 G Street NW, Room 7149 Washington, DC 20548